RETHINK

RETHINK

A Business Manifesto for Cutting Costs and
Boosting Innovation

RIC MERRIFIELD

Vice President, Publisher: Tim Moore
Associate Publisher and Director of Marketing: Amy Neidlinger
Editorial Assistant: Pamela Boland
Operations Manager: Gina Kanouse
Digital Marketing Manager: Julie Phifer
Publicity Manager: Laura Czaja
Assistant Marketing Manager: Megan Colvin
Cover Designer: Brand Navigation
Design Manager: Sandra Schroeder
Managing Editor: Kristy Hart
Senior Project Editor: Lori Lyons
Copy Editor: San Dee Phillips
Proofreader: Kay Hoskin
Senior Indexer: Cheryl Lenser
Senior Compositor: Gloria Schurick
Manufacturing Buyer: Dan Uhrig

FT Press offers excellent discounts on this book when ordered in quantity for bulk purchases or special sales. For more information, please contact U.S. Corporate and Government Sales, 1-800-382-3419, corpsales@pearsontechgroup.com. For sales outside the U.S., please contact International Sales at international@pearson.com.

ISBN-10: 0137031653
ISBN-13: 9780137031658

Pearson Education LTD.
Pearson Education Australia PTY, Limited.
Pearson Education Singapore, Pte. Ltd.
Pearson Education North Asia, Ltd.
Pearson Education Canada, Ltd.
Pearson Educación de Mexico, S.A. de C.V.
Pearson Education—Japan
Pearson Education Malaysia, Pte. Ltd.

Library of Congress Cataloging-in-Publication Data

Merrifield, Eric, 1966-

  Rethink : a business manifesto for cutting costs and boosting innovation / Eric Merrifield.

    p. cm.

  ISBN 978-0-13-703165-8 (hbk. : alk. paper) 1. Management. 2. Strategic planning. 3. Organizational effectiveness. 4. New products. I. Title.

HD31.M3977 2009

  658--dc22

                              2009002465

This book is for my son George.
I am doing everything I can to ensure that you get the education,
and the love, and the experiences that will enable you to do whatever
brings happiness and fulfillment to your life,
something your grandparents Ditty and Papa were so generous to do
for me and your auntie Anne Campbell.

Contents

Introduction 1

ONE

How the "How" Trap Is Trapping You 7

The Cases of the ZIP Code Bandit and the Laggard Laptop 19

If Not Now, When? 21

TWO

The Thinking Behind Rethinking 27

Unit of Analysis: The Task 28

Unit of Analysis: The Worker 31

Unit of Analysis: The Department 32

Unit of Analysis: The Process 33

The New Unit of Analysis: The "What" 34

THREE

First—Identify the "Whats" That Are Truly Valuable 39

Newman's Own, Where More Than Food Has Value 48

How to Rethink Your "Whats" 56

FOUR

Second—Know What You Are (and Aren't) Good At   61

Target, Where the Supply Chain "Whats" Are King   64

Burgerville, Where the Flavor Goes in
and the Garbage Stays Put   66

An Electronics Giant That's Got the Juice   71

How to Rethink Your "Whats"   73

FIVE

Third—Make (and Break) Connections   77

Merck: Beyond the Moat   82

How to Rethink Your "Whats"   88

SIX

Fourth—Understand What Can (and Can't) Be Predicted   91

JetBlue: Storm Warnings   99

How to Rethink Your "Whats"   105

SEVEN

Fifth—Unravel (and Follow) the Rules   109

Matching Laws and "Whats"   114

EIGHT

Revolutionary Rethinking at ING DIRECT   117

ING DIRECT Did What?   131

NINE

Rethinking at Eclipse   133

Eclipse Aviation Did What?   149

TEN

Rethinking at Cranium   151

Cranium Did What?   167

ELEVEN

Morph Again and Again   169

P&G Soars by Morphing Its Innovation "Whats"   186

Key Concepts   193

Conventional "How" Business Views   194

What Is, and Is Not, a "What"   199

Reading a Heat Map   201

Getting to the List of "Whats"   206

A Bit More About Level 1 Maps   209

Level 2 Maps   210

INDEX 213

Acknowledgments

I STARTED WORKING on the materials that led to this book more than five years ago, and along the way a lot of people have in ways large and small contributed to the book and/or the body of work.

At Microsoft, the Module Map team of Norm Judah, David Appel, Liz Davidson, Andi Stark, and Ulrich Homann (who hired me into Microsoft after some convincing from Mike Adams), is where it all started for me. As I created the first version of the Motion methodology, the team at Accelare—including Jack Calhoun, Mark McCormick, Steve McCarthy, and Hannah Will—had a big influence. Then as Motion moved over into a larger consulting offering, Brad Clayton and Chad Corneil joined the team and we further refined the methodology with increasing customer success. That was about the time that Alan Rich started working with me—if it weren't for Alan, I don't know if we ever would have had a heat mapping tool. Michael Dodd has been my patent attorney all this time, and this work is absolutely better because of Michael's guidance.

Mark Baciak was generous enough to move me into a role where I could really focus on writing, while ensuring that my business thinking remained closely aligned with his more technical pursuits. First with the Harvard Business Review work, HBR editor Steve Prokesch and Bob Buday of Bloom Group shepherded that article through many, many revisions—it was great to work with Jack Calhoun again on that, as well as Dennis Stevens from Synaptus who had also contributed to the early methodology work.

Then as focus shifted to the book, Donna Sammons Carpenter, Maurice Coyle, and everyone at Wordworks Inc.—I honestly don't know how many drafts we went through, but it was a genuine pleasure to work with you. As things matured, including a couple of false starts, Tim Moore and Amy Neidlinger at Pearson really pushed hard, which resulted in some changes that are now some of my favorite parts of the book. Lori Lyons was great in the final stages of editing. And to George Murphy of Modo-Group, thank you for your input as well.

Finally—it is my great pleasure and privilege to have a literary agent of the caliber of Helen Rees.

About the Author

RIC MERRIFIELD spent nearly 15 years in various consulting roles helping organizations define and achieve their goals. Since joining Microsoft, Merrifield has spent more than 10,000 hours as a business architect and has filed twelve patent applications all with the goal of helping companies rethink their operating models and get out of the "how" trap described in the pages of this book.

Merrifield recently coauthored "The Next Revolution in Productivity," a June 2008 *Harvard Business Review* article focused on case studies that highlight needs of the organization and the opportunity to rethink business operating models before making major technology changes.

Merrifield is an alumnus of Lakeside School in Seattle and Georgetown University in Washington, D.C.

Introduction

THIS BOOK HAD ITS genesis around the turn of the millennium. At the time, many large companies were adopting two kinds of software programs that transformed the way businesses were run. *Customer relationship management* (CRM) software measured and controlled contacts with customers from marketing, through sales, and into support and other services. *Enterprise resource planning* (ERP) software helped manage inventory, logistics, accounting, and virtually every other aspect of an organization.

We at Microsoft were aware that the CRM and ERP programs were coloring companies' decisions about which computer systems to buy—and there we were sitting on the sidelines. So we decided to create our own business application software. There was one small problem: We lacked in-depth knowledge of our potential customers' operations.

The team that was assembled to explore this *terra incognita* suggested the creation of a detailed map of a hypothetical company's essential business activities. It began with an outline of an archetypal business' five top activities—or as we initially called them, "capabilities"—that included the following:

1. Create Products and Services

2. Generate Demand

3. Deliver Products and Services

4. Plan and Manage the Business

5. Manage Collaboration

The more the team examined these high-level capabilities, the more it saw them as overall categories encompassing hundreds of lesser, though still vital, capabilities that it set down in descending order. Under "Generate Demand," for example, were listed several major capabilities, including "Market Products and Services," which, in turn, sat atop a group of capabilities that included "Manage Marketing"—and so it went.

Eventually, the team had a list of literally hundreds of universal capabilities that covered about 80 percent of all business activities and constituted an entire nomenclature for every company anywhere on earth. When presented in map form, the list filled a six-by-six-foot poster that, ironically, looked like a giant blowup of a computer chip. It described not just a company, but the workings of everything and everyone connected with the business.

The map served admirably as a means of orienting Microsoft salespeople to the complex operations of potential customers. But it also took on a life of its own.

It turned out that the map, tailored to take into account the differences between industries, gave the company leaders we called on a unique overview of their operations. Laying out their capabilities in discrete, interconnected chunks—LEGO bricks, if you will—made it much simpler for them to spot and eliminate duplications and determine which elements of their operations to keep and which to outsource or automate.

In what proved to be a happy coincidence, the map emerged just as two major developments—Web 2.0 and service-oriented architecture (SOA)—were starting to revolutionize business management. The advent of Web 2.0 helped the Internet evolve from a mere collection of Web sites to a complete computing platform. Now, we could create Web-based software applications and operate them for our customers. Companies communicated and shifted work as never before. At the same time, SOA was beginning to gain momentum, making it possible to see the relationships between and among the hundreds of capabilities within a company—and with its suppliers and customers as well. Suddenly, business leaders could automate, share, outsource, even sell one or another element of their operations without going through the messy analytics of interfaces and integration.

The power of the map, the third piece of the puzzle, was now even more of a boon to business performance. It provided the words to cut through the proprietary languages that are so pervasive at many companies (ours included), and it served to fully unlock the potential of SOA and the Internet.

Since its first appearance, the map has grown and evolved. The master list of typical capabilities, for example, has been substantially expanded. Beyond that, the basic concept of a capability has been enlarged and made part of the overarching new approach to management that is the topic of this book. These ideas received their first public airing in a June 2008 *Harvard Business Review* article written by the author of this book together with Jack Calhoun of Accelare and Dennis Stevens of Synaptus.

And as the approach has evolved, the term "capability" has been more precisely refined. Now the focus is on the desired outcomes of an activity—*what* it does as opposed to *how* it is done. So instead of speaking of capabilities in the pages ahead, they are referred to as "whats." The distinction is important, particularly because management theory in recent decades has focused so strongly on how-oriented programs such as reengineering and Six Sigma. It has also helped make the approach basic enough to be understood and applied by employees at every level of a company.

Microsoft's product philosophy has undergone a major evolution as well. Today, we view the future of our corporate customers as being tied to the interaction of local software and Internet services; the architectural-design power of SOA is wedded to the managerial power of Web-based *software-as-a-service* (SaaS). We call the combination Software Plus Services, or S+S.

Information technology, per se, does not receive a great deal of attention in this book. That's because IT is a means to an end rather than an end in and of itself—a "how" rather than a "what"—and this book is essentially about helping leaders to better comprehend and manage their "whats." From a Microsoft point of view, that is a devoutly wished-for consummation, because if our customers don't know what their companies require, we have a hard time helping them decide how best to get there.

As these words are being written, the economic climate in the United States has taken a distinctly worrisome turn. A recession represents yet another challenge for business leaders already facing cruel competition, globalization, and the vagaries of ever more fickle and demanding customers. This book offers a new, yet proven, approach that has enabled many companies to achieve vastly greater efficiency and flexibility. May it do the same for you, too.

Ron Markezich, Corporate Vice President,
Microsoft Online Services

ONE

How the "How" Trap Is Trapping You

"It is not the strongest of the species that survive,
or the most intelligent, but the ones most responsive to change."

–Charles Darwin

THE HOME-IMPROVEMENT colossus had been the fastest-growing retailer in U.S. history, its revenues doubling every two or three years for more than a decade. But by 2000, Home Depot was showing signs of wear. So the board of directors filled the top job with a high-powered fixer-upper, Robert L. Nardelli, who had proven his mettle as a senior executive at General Electric.

The new chairman and CEO thought he knew just what Home Depot needed, a jolt of new-found efficiency. He simplified processes, slashed costs, and invested $1 billion in new technology while doubling the number of stores. He promised investors that the company would reach new heights of sales and profitability, and he delivered: Between 2000 and his departure in 2006, annual revenues soared from $45 billion to nearly $80 billion, and profits doubled. But amid that success, Nardelli also came close to destroying the single, most-important advantage the company possessed.

Since its founding in 1978, Home Depot had triumphed over its competitors because of the friendly, helpful environment in its stores. Salespeople, backed by innovative, hands-off managers, eagerly answered customers' questions and shared their home-improvement knowledge and experience. As a result, weekend novices learned a new vocabulary (a Phillips screwdriver, for example, is not a cocktail) and became skilled do-it-yourselfers and steadfast Home Depot customers.

In pursuit of savings, Nardelli slashed employees' hours to the point that many seasoned people quit; they were replaced by less-knowledgeable and less-committed part-timers. He also stripped store managers of their traditional autonomy. Before long, Home Depot had devolved into a generic big-box outlet run by nervous functionaries micromanaging unhelpful, uninterested salespeople. Meanwhile, Home Depot's chief rival, Lowe's, was staffing its stores with just the kind of outgoing, caring men and women who had originally given Home Depot its edge.

In 2001, Home Depot and Lowe's held identical rankings among specialty retailers on the University of Michigan's American Customer Satisfaction Index (ACSI). By 2005, Lowe's was second only to Costco, and Home Depot was at the bottom of the list. Although revenues increased during Nardelli's reign (largely because of store expansion), customer satisfaction took a nosedive. From 2000 to 2006, Home Depot's ACSI score was a mere 1.7 out of a possible 100. Meanwhile, Lowe's same-store sales growth averaged nearly three times that of Home Depot, and investors paid heed: Home Depot's stock price was flat between 2000 and 2007, while Lowe's shares jumped more than 200 percent.

In January 2007, the board of directors handed Nardelli his walking papers. By conventional standards, he had done everything right—cutting costs, improving processes, and increasing efficiency and productivity. His mistake? Falling victim to the "how" trap. Nardelli had focused almost entirely on improving the efficiency (read: cost) of the work being done rather than on the purpose of that work. In other words, he trained his sights on the "how" of any given activity rather than on the "what," the outcome it sought to achieve. In Home Depot's case, the crucial "what" was helping customers to find the right product, that being the capability that drove sales.

Nardelli's error is all too common. Leaders tend to devote their energies to thinking about the details, thereby missing the big picture. We invest our time in improving job efficiency without stopping to rethink the value of the job itself. And that means we fail to ask, and answer, some essential questions: How important is a particular activity to the company's goals? How well is it performing in that context? Should it be given greater attention and resources? Should it be automated? Outsourced? Or completely eliminated because its work is being duplicated elsewhere in the organization?

Our mistakes accumulate—and not without good reason. For one thing, we spend our days in the office coping with immediate concerns. In today's perilous economic environment, there's precious little time for anything else. Moreover, management theory in recent years has pointed us toward a focus on process, on how efficiently a job is done as opposed to what the job is supposed to accomplish.

Yet most of us haven't rethought which of our activities are most important to our companies, which are succeeding, which are borderline or even redundant. Indeed, until now, there has been no way to accurately and efficiently rethink and measure all these "whats" because we have been caught in the "how" trap, a pervasive and perverse human condition that allows us to sidestep blame for failing to reach our organization's potential.

Consider this mundane but illuminating example: Back in the summer of 2008, with the price of gasoline soaring to obscene heights, a friend of mine had a kind of epiphany. Once each day, she drove to her favorite park to walk her golden retriever. She never really thought about the route she was taking; it was just how she got to the park. Then one August day, after an eye-popping visit to a gas station, she decided it was time to cut back on her driving. It had become just too expensive.

The daily trip to the park was her first target. She spent an hour or two poring over a map looking for a better route, and, eventually, she found one. It was shorter, skirted traffic, and was burdened by only a few lights. My friend tried the new route over the next week, and it did save her a few minutes of driving and a few cents worth of gasoline. Nevertheless, she was disappointed with the results.

Then she had a brainstorm. Instead of struggling to improve the "how" of getting to her favorite park, she drastically rethought the situation at hand—the "what" that she hoped to accomplish. She spread out her map and began looking for other suitable parks much closer to her house. Sure enough, she found one. Her new destination wasn't as big or as woodsy as her favorite, but the dog was happy—and over a week's time, she could calculate her fuel savings in dollars.

A particularly memorable example of someone putting on his rethinking cap to escape the "how" trap was Oregon high-jumper Dick Fosbury. Until Fosbury came along, athletes attempted to clear the high bar by running face forward toward it and using an open scissor-style jumping motion, a technique not unlike the way hurdlers run and jump over their barriers. Faced with the "what" of **Jump-Over-the-Bar** and needing to achieve the best possible height to win, Fosbury introduced a method that was almost the opposite of the then-standard technique: He would run toward the bar at great speed and then, just prior to jumping, he would twist his body to put his back to the bar so he could "flop" over head first. By rethinking his approach, Fosbury won a gold medal in the 1968 Summer Olympics in Mexico City, setting a new standard "how" for accomplishing the "what" of **Jump-Over-the-Bar**.

My work has shown that our world is a treasure trove of Fosbury Flops waiting to be discovered, and the only thing holding people back is the rethinking required to get out of the "how" trap.

Business leaders' final destinations may differ, but all face similar problems on the road to finding a better way of accomplishing a task. And if they seek advice from the people who actually do the work of their companies, the answers will tend to be more confusing than helpful. That's because employees and managers typically respond as my dog-walking friend did at first; they think of their jobs in terms of how they do them rather than what they are intended to accomplish. So they may recount the work-flow process steps and any technology used, relying on descriptions that are chock full of company-specific terminology and that vary according to the person being asked. Ask five different people, and you'll get five different explanations—all accurate in their way but a product of the subjective, limited views of each spokesperson.

Where, then, do managers or leaders turn if they want to intelligently and efficiently boost productivity? They have a raft of subjective perspectives about the work but lack the clear and stable view of their organizations that they need to accurately assess the cost, value, risk, or impact of acting (or not acting) on a problem or opportunity. And with multiple perspectives to sort through, they inevitably find themselves stuck in a long, arduous, and argumentative process before they can arrive at organizational consensus on priorities and actions that might or might not be the best answer.

The approach presented in these pages enables business leaders to rethink—rise above that clutter of "hows" and consider the "whats," the desired outcomes of an organization's thousands of activities. The key is to just stop wasting time and effort thinking about the "hows." After all, as we know, they are subjective, unreliable, and diversionary—they blind you to big-picture realities. And when you ditch the "hows" to concentrate on the "whats," you are rethinking, and rethinking is what can allow you to reach precise, reasoned decisions about the resources you should invest in any given aspect of your operations.

Some people believe that the practice of business is a blend of art and science, and that any attempt to deconstruct a company into its elemental constituents is misguided if not impossible. My research has led me to a different conclusion: The activities of every business can and should be reduced to a fundamental, objective view of the totality of the work the company does. And in my research, I have identified the "whats" that comprise 80 percent of every company's outcomes, no matter the industry.

When you rethink—forgetting about the "hows" to concentrate on the "whats"—you are creating an easily understood table of your company's essential components. And when you see them laid out in their logical sequence, you can determine the organizational value of each "what."

The process and its outcome reminds me of a problem I run into when I go trout fishing under a bright, azure sky. The sun's reflections make it almost impossible to see the fish swimming below the surface. When I put on polarized sunglasses, though, I can look deeper into the water, spotting what I hope to catch.

Just so, your rethought list of "whats" opens your eyes to the deep-down workings of your company presented in orderly fashion. It makes you indifferent to how these elements have been traditionally arranged within the organization, freeing you to concentrate on what really matters—outcomes. After your "whats" have been defined, you can step back and determine whether and to what degree each of them contributes to your enterprise's success. Then, depending upon your findings, you can eliminate some, outsource others, and reorder the ones that remain, just like those plug-and-play monitors and printers that arrive ready to use. You have escaped from the "how" trap. That's the beauty of rethinking.

Consider what happens when an insurance agent phones headquarters to assess a new customer's policy application and get a premium quote. A manager at the home office, using some sort of actuarial algorithm in a spreadsheet, comes up with a quote and sends it to the agent via e-mail. Ask that insurance agent "what" he does, and chances are he'll say he makes a phone call, waits, and receives an e-mail. He's caught in the "how" trap. But if that agent were to rethink and focus on his "whats," he'd see that the transaction in question breaks down into these desired outcomes:

- **Request-Customer-Premium**

- **Calculate-Customer-Premium**

- **Prepare-Customer-Quote**

- **Customer-Quote-Communication**

If the insurance firm's rivals are stealing market share, and if its managers cannot rethink what they do—that is, if they are caught in the "how" trap—they typically search for an explanation and a solution in such minutiae as the length of time an agent spends calling the home office or the efficiency of the company's e-mail system. Their tunnel vision can lead their organization to undertake expensive, disruptive process "improvements"—changing telephone providers, let's say, or implementing new e-mail systems—that might or might not succeed.

If, however, the company's leaders can rethink and examine the "whats," they can have the advantage of seeing the operation in its entirety, thus illuminating a pathway for getting to the root issues. They might ask: Should the agent be empowered to come up with the premium quote himself? Or should the task be turned over to a vendor?

Here's another example that points up the value of rethinking. Remember what it used to be like to check in for a flight? You had to wait in long lines, inching your way toward a counter where a harried airline employee presided. He was responsible for a host of steps; among them

- Examining identifications
- Checking reservations
- Processing payments
- Assigning seats
- Issuing boarding passes
- Issuing luggage tickets

That process might still be the norm today if someone hadn't rethought check-in procedures. That sainted someone realized that flight check-in consists of just four distinct desired outcomes:

- A completed security check
- A confirmed reservation

- An issued boarding pass

- A completed luggage check-in

When the desired outcomes were understood, there was the realization that even though there was still a need for the original "how" (gate agent) because of some of the "what" exceptions, when it comes to the core "whats" it really doesn't matter

- Who does the work (passenger, even)

- How many steps there are (about four in the case of the airport kiosk and roughly the same on the Web, but more when talking to the airline employee)

- What technology is used (Internet, kiosk, whatever is used by the airline employee)

- Even where it happens (hotel, airport kiosk, home, and so on)

Each of those is a "how" and checking in at the airport is a good example of how the airline industry got out of a "how" trap.

Technology has given business leaders new abilities and options, and it is at the heart of the approach set forth in this book. Rethinking and focusing on "whats" allows you to choose the most cost-effective ways to achieve core goals and increase efficiency and productivity, free of the "how" trap.

THE CASES OF THE ZIP CODE BANDIT
AND THE LAGGARD LAPTOP

Not long ago, the chief information officer of a large, well-known manufacturing company asked my colleagues and me to help him with a problem. Having gone through scores of mergers and acquisitions, his company had piled redundancy upon redundancy over the years until some operations were nearly sclerotic—and this despite having been reengineered. Eager to save money, the CIO wanted to rethink his organization, so we started with the data system that enabled the company to verify its customers' shipping and billing addresses using their ZIP Codes. He said he knew for a fact that two separate parts of the company were each paying the same supplier for the same ZIP Code information. Fired up by the prospect of saving $2.5 million, he was eager to unplug the redundant ZIP Code data.

At our suggestion, the CIO sent out a mass e-mail to every corner of his company to see if there might be any other redundant ZIP Code purchases. Sure enough, one turned up, and the annual charge for the same data was almost identical to the other two. Quite a coincidence, we thought, if not suspiciously odd. So we asked to see the invoices. Guess what? The same provider had sold the same data to our client three times.

Now we were really curious, so we asked the CIO to find out how many of the company's various comptrollers had remitted payments to this particular provider of ZIP Code data. The answer that came back was 12.

The annual cost for each of these ranged from $1.8 million to more than $3 million—for the exact same data. By this time, of course, the CIO was furious with this unscrupulous supplier, but, as happens with many large organizations where "what" elements go undefined and their intersections remain unrecognized, our client had made it all too easy for his company to be taken advantage of. Minor variations in usage across different divisions were used to justify some of the purchases, creating classic "how" traps that often mask opportunities to leverage a best practice or consolidate people, process, and technology "hows."

It took us nearly four months to eliminate the 11 redundant systems and get a new one up and running that met our specifications. When we were finished, the CIO found himself with an extra $40 million, more than 15 times the savings he had initially been hoping for. It worked out to an average $2.7 million for each redundant system, plus the capital expenditures for the no-longer-needed supporting hardware, and an estimated savings of $100,000 a year for each of 63 technology staffers who could be otherwise deployed.

In another example, Toshiba's customers were boiling about the pace of laptop repairs. It typically took two weeks from the time a customer dropped off a machine until it came back. By rethinking and focusing on the "whats," the company discovered that the actual repair time averaged less than an hour; most of the remaining time was eaten up in transporting the computer from the store to the technician and back to the store. When Toshiba deconstructed the problem, which turned out to be external and logistical rather than internal and knowledge-based, it eliminated the **Repair-Product** "what" and turned it over to the logistics unit, because the majority of the "whats" were related to logistics anyway. Among those "whats" were the following:

- **Collect-Product**

- **Transport-Product-to-Warehouse**

- **Deliver-Parts-to-Warehouse**

- **Return-Product-to-Customer**

The result? Laptop repair time was shortened to a few days and customer satisfaction improved.

IF NOT NOW, WHEN?

Never has there been a more important time to continually improve your company's efficiency and productivity. The current economic downturn has forced us all to be more conscious of the need to husband our resources and leverage to our greatest advantage those in which we invest. For companies to survive in this harrowing new environment, they must, as noted earlier, be constantly improving their efficiency and productivity. And for that to happen, they are going to have to avoid the "how" trap, rethink and focus on their "whats," and become a collection of plug-and-play operations. This book is a primer on that new and necessary strategy. Chapters 3 through 7, in particular, guide you in rethinking and managing your organization's "whats" and reaching informed decisions about which of them should be enhanced and which should be eliminated.

- Chapter 2, "The Thinking Behind Rethinking": The groundbreaking operational improvements of the last century have been driven by advances in process management and technology— and by historic changes in the unit of analysis. These changes, as this chapter describes, have paved the way for a revolutionary new operations design technique.

- Chapter 3, "First—Identify the 'Whats' That Are Truly Valuable": Step one in rethinking is to identify and analyze them to determine what contribution each makes to your company's progress. The greatest value often comes from an unexpected quarter, and this chapter shows you how to spot it.

- Chapter 4, "Second—Know What You Are (and Aren't) Good At": After you identify your most valuable "whats," you must determine how well they perform. Some useful and easily applied approaches to measuring performance are presented and amplified in this chapter, using company examples that include Target, Hon Hai, and Burgerville. I also get an assist from Michael Jordan.

- Chapter 5, "Third—Make (and Break) Connections": After you identify the "whats" that generate value and how they perform, you need to pause. Before you can start rethinking and making changes to your "whats," you need to understand how the "whats" relate to one another. Otherwise, you might jettison a nonperformer only to set off a destructive chain reaction among its high-performing but dependent neighbors. This chapter shows you how to make those decisions.

- Chapter 6, "Fourth—Understand What Can (and Can't) Be Predicted": When you identify the "whats" that create value, and determine their performance and interconnections, you need to figure out how your company and its customers, suppliers, and partners are likely to react to the plug-and-play changes you have in mind. This chapter gives you practical advice on mapping this territory.

- Chapter 7, "Fifth—Unravel (and Follow) The Rules": You have reached the final level of decision making before you can begin plugging and playing. In this chapter, you learn how to align your key "whats" with the complex maze of federal, state, and even foreign regulations.

- In Chapters 8, "Revolutionary Rethinking at ING DIRECT," 9, "Rethinking at Eclipse," and 10, "Rethinking at Cranium," I paint three full-scale portraits of plug-and-play management: ING DIRECT, Eclipse, and Cranium. Particularly in the current economic climate, the stories of ING DIRECT and Eclipse are vivid illustrations of organizations breaking free of traditional "how" traps and successfully cutting costs, while, at the same time, introducing breakthrough innovations.

- Chapter 11, "Morph Again and Again": Winning companies, this chapter argues, know how to rethink and reconfigure their "whats" to adapt to the unending changes of the marketplace. My exemplars are Amazon.com and Proctor & Gamble, two organizations that have plugged and played their way out of "how" traps through one dramatic change after another.

- Key Concepts: I've included this section as a useful quick reference to the basic ideas in this book to help you in your rethinking journey.

In the chapters ahead, you find familiar problems and unfamiliar, impressively successful solutions. They reflect a powerful new approach to the management of your enterprise—a way you can escape the "how" trap. The chapters are, in effect, a guide to an important, field-tested technique for achieving major improvements in your company's efficiency and productivity. I think you will agree that my method is tailor-made for this age of escalating competition and extreme economic uncertainty.

TWO

The Thinking Behind Rethinking

"If you don't know where you are going, you might wind up someplace else."

–Yogi Bera

WHEN BUSINESSPEOPLE talk about the extraordinary productivity gains of the last decade, the lion's share of credit typically goes to technology. I protest. Although it's true that major advances in the machines and software that gather, process, and distribute information have made possible whole new ways of organizing work in a company, business productivity owes just as much to operational design theory. In fact, innovative design concepts such as the time-and-motion studies of the early 1900s, the *total quality management* (TQM) programs of the '80s, and the reengineering initiatives of the '90s led to enormous gains in business efficiency.

Today, we're poised for another productivity breakthrough, but to take full advantage of it, we need a new and more powerful approach. This book offers precisely that, a groundbreaking way to lift productivity by maximizing the value of your company's "whats."

UNIT OF ANALYSIS: THE TASK

In his landmark 1776 book, *The Wealth of Nations*, Scottish philosopher and economist Adam Smith called attention to a revolutionary development in the nature of work in his day. Machines were just beginning to replace manual labor, and most goods were still made by hand, with each worker performing all the operations needed to make the final

product. Smith described a far more efficient proce-
dure at a pin factory:

> *One man draws out the wire,*
> *another straights it, a third cuts it,*
> *a fourth points it, a fifth grinds it*
> *at the top for receiving the head; to*
> *make the head requires two or three*
> *distinct operations; to put it on, is a*
> *peculiar business, to whiten the pins*
> *is another; it is even a trade by itself*
> *to put them into the paper; and the*
> *important business of making a pin*
> *is, in this manner, divided into about*
> *eighteen distinct operations....*

When one worker was responsible for all those
tasks, Smith wrote, he could produce only 20 pins
in a day. But if the 18 tasks were distributed among
10 people, they could turn out 48,000 pins a day.

Underlying Smith's epiphany about the division of
labor was a concept that is central to an understanding of process improvement theory. Any research
effort will necessarily require the researcher to
focus on one or another element of the entity being
studied. That element is known as the *unit of analysis*. For example, if you look at urban architecture,
the unit of analysis might be an individual building,
a city block, or a whole neighborhood. Choosing
the unit of analysis is the student's critical decision,

whether the topic is a city's architecture or a factory floor. That one decision determines the nature and the scope of the results.

In the case of the pin factory, Adam Smith's unit of analysis was the worker's task. His choice led him to discover that productivity soared when a worker focused on just one task, because he could perform it faster and better than a worker who was creating a pin all by himself and trying to master many tasks at once.

In selecting a unit of analysis, you need to make sure it's homogeneous. That is, the activities included have to be closely related, either by physical proximity—people working side by side on an assembly line, let's say—or by the need to share information. If two activities can be coordinated better when information is communicated quickly from one to the other, those activities belong within the same unit of analysis. But at the pin factory, the only means of transferring information from worker to worker was by word of mouth or hand-written notes. Workers had little or no information about the status of the tasks that came before or after theirs, or what happened to the goods when they left the factory. There was no feedback of customer complaints, for example. Thus, the unit of analysis could not extend beyond the individual worker's task.

UNIT OF ANALYSIS: THE WORKER

A century after Adam Smith advocated breaking an individual's work into specific tasks, thereby turning generalists into specialists, a new business specialty, the operational improvement expert, was emerging. The most influential of these experts was a Germantown, Pennsylvania, mechanical engineer named Frederick Winslow Taylor.

In the 1890s, Taylor began advising manufacturers of steel and paper on how to improve factory output. Born into an affluent, educated, and progressive Quaker family, Taylor believed the key to productivity improvements was in rigorously studying every aspect of every worker's job. Accordingly, he timed workers' actions to the hundredth of a second, searching for wasted motion. He believed that there was only one "best way" to do any job and that managers (not workers) were the only ones who could determine what that was.

Taylor's time-and-motion studies made individuals the locus of operational improvement; his unit of analysis was not the task, but the worker. By 1911, when he published his path-breaking book, *The Principles of Scientific Management*, the technology for moving information from worker to worker in a factory had not improved much from Adam Smith's day. Word of mouth was still the preferred medium.

UNIT OF ANALYSIS: THE DEPARTMENT

By the mid-1960s, 50 years after Taylor's death, a revolution in information technology was ushering in a whole new approach to operations improvement. Giant computers began appearing in corporate offices, some of them requiring a whole room of their own. The flow of information among workers in the same department went from a word-of-mouth trickle to a torrent, with all the workers in a department viewing the same material simultaneously and acting upon technology in concert.

Now the unit of operational analysis shifted from the individual worker to the department, a collection of computer-connected employees focused on highly related tasks—the accounting department, for example, sent invoices and paid bills. Leading the charge were operations consultants such as John Diebold, author of the much-admired 1952 book, *Automation*. Diebold urged businesses to use computers to coordinate the work of people within the same department.

The Bowery Savings Bank of New York was among Diebold's adherents, eager for the process improvements brought by his consulting firm. For the first time, computer-linked tellers at all the branches could access the account information of every customer. Now customers could make deposits and withdrawals at any Bowery Savings branch, not just the one at which they opened their accounts.

Diebold also advised newspaper companies to replace their typewriters with computer terminals, allowing workers in the same department—newsroom reporters and editors, for instance—to improve the news production work flow. (The news business being traditionally hidebound, most newspapers ignored his advice until the 1980s.)

The high cost of transmitting computerized information through the telecommunications networks of the 1960s and '70s meant that most corporate computer networks remained local. Workers in a department such as accounting or customer service could be linked together by a computer and communications system if they were housed in the same building, or, as in the case of Bowery Savings, if they were in the same city. But connecting people across offices—especially those in different states or overseas—was economically prohibitive for all but the most critical business activities. As a result, the unit of operational analysis in the 1960s and '70s was largely a department within an organization.

UNIT OF ANALYSIS: THE PROCESS
The information technology revolution of the early 1990s dramatically lowered the cost of computers and communications, making the flow of voluminous information across departments economically feasible. Computing power that had cost millions of dollars in the 1960s—the "big iron" mainframes—

could be purchased for just thousands of dollars by the 1990s. Telecommunications prices fell dramatically as well, cutting the cost of connecting computers across long distances.

With these two advances, it became technologically and financially feasible for even far-flung workers in many departments of a company to work off the same information. Customer information possessed by the finance department in Chicago, for instance, was also accessible to a salesperson in New York.

Early in the decade, a new wave of operational improvement theorists such as James Champy and Michael Hammer realized that this new capability allowed work to be reorganized across departments or functions. Thus, the cross-functional process became the unit of analysis for operational improvement. Champy and Hammer called their operations-improvement method *reengineering*, and it sparked a revolution in productivity. Another revolution, this time in software known as *enterprise resource planning* (ERP), followed shortly thereafter.

THE NEW UNIT OF ANALYSIS: THE "WHAT"

Today, many companies continue to use reengineering to achieve productivity gains. But over the last decade, the confluence of three major advances in information technology has set the stage for a new, more powerful unit of analysis—not the tasks performed by a worker or a department, the "hows," but the desired outcome of those tasks. Today, the key to increased productivity is the rethinking of the "whats." The approach to performance improvement espoused in this book has been successfully adopted by dozens of companies, some of which you will read about in the chapters ahead. It fits hand-in-glove with the new technologies that are so essential to the future of business.

The rapid rise of the World Wide Web in the second half of the 1990s, combined with the dot-com era's proliferation of cheap bandwidth—powerful communications networks for transmitting a tidal wave of digital information around the world—has made it inexpensive for the departments of a global company to be plugged into the same information anywhere around the world. The high-cost private telecommunications companies that previously kept businesses digitally connected have been supplanted by a low-cost public computer network.

Yet another key technological advance has been the rapid growth in the number of business activities that are now software-based, particularly those aimed at gathering, manipulating, and processing information. Connecting telephone calls, for example, previously required thousands of telephone operators who diligently plugged their wires into huge switchboards. A half-century later, that activity is totally automated by means of software. In a similar manner, payroll-processing software used by such companies as ADP and Paychex has replaced work that used to be performed by tens of thousands of payroll clerks.

Given these developments, achieving major productivity improvement now depends in part on reducing the cost of the new software and the computers that run it—a bill that reaches into the billions of dollars at some companies. The Internet offers a solution. It allows corporate divisions to share the same software inexpensively across great distances by using applications that reside on the Web—or to use a more current term, the cloud—and corporate networks rather than on individual computers. But for a sharing solution to work properly, the software must be based upon a common set of design principles, and those principles are still being developed using *service-oriented architecture* (SOA) and *software-as-a-service* (SaaS).

Still another requirement must be met for Web-based software sharing to achieve its potential: The various and varied operating divisions within a company need to define their business operations in a common way. If five divisions of a company are to plug into one accounts receivable software application on a corporate intranet, each division must define the work in the same way.

My approach to rethinking an organization and considering its "whats," which this book lays out, fills that need. Now managers in each division of a company can agree on how to define the work of, say, collecting customers' payments in terms of the outcome—the "what"—that the employees are trying to achieve rather than in terms of "how" they perform the tasks that produce that outcome.

In the following chapters, I show how companies large and small have adopted the rethought "what" approach not just as a way to adapt to the demands of Web-based sharing, but also to achieve greater productivity and efficiency. It succeeds because it gives company leaders a detailed, actionable view of the workings of their organizations—the activities that need to be streamlined, improved, outsourced, or dropped altogether.

By rethinking and adopting the "what" as a unit of analysis, organizations are presenting a challenge for leaders and managers, particularly those who have spent their careers on operational improvement. It is not at all easy for even the most operationally efficient among them to reorient their focus away from the "hows." Nor, truth be told, will the increased transparency of your company make your job any easier. Distinguishing a single "what" from a series of "hows" is simple enough, but you still have to make tough decisions about where to put your resources. The following chapters take you through the steps involved in adopting the "what" approach and rethinking your business to make it work in a plug-and-play world. Just ahead you encounter the first crucial step—determining which "whats" are contributing value and which are not.

Let's get to it.

THREE

First—Identify the "Whats" That Are Truly Valuable

> "Price is what you pay.
> Value is what you get."
>
> –Warren Buffett

HAVING MADE THE decision to rethink your "whats" and use them as your unit of analysis, you're now ready to begin the process of identifying and examining their desired outcomes, and judging how to improve their performance. To start, you need to determine which "whats" are truly generating high value for your company.

Just to be clear, when I describe a given "what" as having "high value," I mean that it is contributing to overall performance or differentiating your company from its rivals in some significant way. For example, ship-product might be a high-value "what" in your company because its outstanding performance sets your company apart from its competitors. Or even if its performance is nothing special, it might provide high value simply because it satisfies customers—and customer satisfaction helps keep costs constant.

You will want to pinpoint "whats" having high value so that you can focus your "how" improvement efforts where they will count the most. You also need to determine their current performance levels and why they perform as they do. Don't even think about changing a high-value "what" unless you possess an in-depth understanding of the cause of its performance. Is it the people, the process, the technology, or some blend of those "hows?"

As you move through the rethinking process, prepare to encounter some surprises. Your most valuable "whats" might be those you least expect. Witness the experience of Alcoa, the giant manufacturer of aluminum and aluminum products based in Pittsburgh, Pennsylvania.

In doing the research for this book, I came across an article in an old issue of *Industry Week* magazine that began: "August 9, 1991, will be remembered as the day the world's largest aluminum producer bought its ticket to the 21st century." Those words heralded the decision by then-chairman and CEO Paul O'Neill to rejuvenate the wheezing, old colossus he had recently been chosen to lead. O'Neill lived up to the promise, showing an intuitive understanding of the need to rethink the company in terms of its "whats," not its "hows," and he chose an unlikely "what" to galvanize the work of Alcoa's 63,000 employees. As a result, the company's efficiency surged, value and bottom-line performance soared, and the stock price followed suit.

A fan of new technology, O'Neill nevertheless shunned the high-flown, high-tech "whats" and focused instead on something seemingly marginal: safety. It was a choice that struck other business leaders as odd, to say the least. But safety, O'Neill declared, "is the most important leading indicator of how good a company is or could be."

Safety?

All too many leaders accept job injuries and illnesses as just another cost of doing business, but O'Neill wasn't about to ignore something that took such a heavy human and financial toll. He rethought the importance of safety at Alcoa—or in our parlance, the "whats" of a safe, zero-injury workplace—seeing them as the lightning bolt that could electrify his workforce. Some of those "whats" included the following:

- **Confirm-Safe-Work-Environment**, which eliminated certain "hows" such as talking on a conference call on a cell phone while driving.

- **Apply-Safety-Clothing**, an explicit "what" that made sure people were given hard hats and thermal protective gear to do their jobs.

- **Assign-Qualified-Resource-to-Task**, a "what" applicable to roles that require a test or a certification; when enforced, this "what" reduces the risk of putting the wrong person in a role.

O'Neill was—and is—a crusty Missourian with degrees in economics and public administration. Before joining Alcoa, he had chalked up 15 years of experience in Washington, DC, as a rising federal official and 11 more at International Paper, where he became president in 1985. Two years later, he was wooed and won by Alcoa.

O'Neill's post-Alcoa career was famously dominated by his turbulent two years as President George W. Bush's first secretary of the U.S. Treasury Department. He strongly opposed the president's tax-cut policies, and after resigning his position, he publicly and presciently called the president's economic program irresponsible, charging that the administration's policy decisions were blindly political.

O'Neill also recalled that, early on, Bush had dismissed his proposal to make the federal government "the safest workplace in the world." But he forged ahead, trying his safety ideas on the Treasury. "While I was there, we reduced the injury rate 50 percent," he later noted.

Though clearly not a politician, O'Neill treasured results. Back when he began rethinking Alcoa, he insisted on changing the company's priorities. Out went a command-and-control structure with its rigidities and turf wars; in came a dedication to customers and business units. The frontline took precedence—not Pittsburgh headquarters, not management, not O'Neill himself. The then-current industry mantra called for "continuous improvement," but that wasn't enough for O'Neill (probably because he knew that blind continuous improvement amounts to nothing less than an exercise in paving the cow path). He demanded "rapid, quantum-leap improvement." Within two years, he decreed, Alcoa would erase 80 percent of the gap between its operating performance and industry benchmarks.

O'Neill cleared that bar like a champion high jumper practicing the Fosbury Flop, using safety to catapult the company up and over its rivals. When he arrived, Alcoa's lost-workday incidence rate was 1.44 per 100 employees, already far superior to the average of 4.73 for all U.S. manufacturers. Eighteen months after his edict, the company's lost-workday rate had dropped to 0.75 on its way to still lower levels—this in an enterprise full of dangerous work like mining and smelting. (The success story continues: In 2007, 89.9 percent of the company's 316 locations lost no workdays whatsoever.)

O'Neill drove the "whats" connected to the no-worker-injuries metric so hard that it became embedded in the minds of employees. He made sure that all managers at all levels were on board, of course, but he equally stressed the role of frontline employees as partners and facilitators on the plant floor. "You can't get good safety results by beating the hell out of people," he said. Employees themselves had to scope out hazards and solutions. They operated the potentially dangerous equipment and understood better than the higher-ups how it should be designed and used to improve safety. O'Neill urged factory workers to speak out and they did, offering valuable safety ideas and strengthening Alcoa's culture along the way.

The company's intense focus on safety produced a significant boost in employee morale—and, in turn, business performance. The fact that O'Neill and Alcoa cared so much about employees' safety, and devoted so much time, energy, and money to improving it, clearly created enormous goodwill among the rank-and-file. For those who think a bigger paycheck is the only avenue to boosting employee attitudes and loyalty, the Alcoa story shows that it ain't necessarily so.

Throughout the process of rethinking at Alcoa however, O'Neill never lost his interest in technology. He saw to it that Alcoa embraced the Internet early, using it to connect all parts of the company and to keep employees abreast of developments. This sharing of information was another way to make people feel more involved in the enterprise and committed to its overall performance. O'Neill also ordered that computer-based statistical tools be used to compare the safety performance of various plants, to "tease out of the data those things you ought to be focusing on." When "those things" were identified, he reasoned, they could be shared online "so that people don't have to learn the lessons over and over again." He recognized that different plants had different strengths that would be essential to achieving his desired overall safety outcome of zero injuries. In other words, the key was to drill down below the metric of no-worker-injuries metric to find the "whats" in place at each plant.

Gradually, the entire organization bought into O'Neill's goal of zero-worker injuries. "Safety is not an option," a company manager told *Occupational Hazards* magazine in 2002. "It's part of everything we do." And "everything" extended well beyond the standard precautions like wearing protective equipment and stressing ergonomic design. It also included a prohibition that is only now gaining currency in several states and municipalities: Alcoa employees are forbidden from using cell phones while driving on company business, which, of course, is a "how" that increases the risk of a metric of no-worker-injuries.

During the O'Neill era, Alcoa's annual revenues jumped 1,400 percent, to $23 billion from $1.5 billion. It was no accident that the CEO's dedication to safety created efficiencies that boosted Alcoa's financial results and its stock price. A retired Alcoa director, Donald S. Perkins, summed up O'Neill's legacy: "His major impact has been to run an Old Economy company as though it were a New Economy company." Put another way, by rethinking Alcoa, O'Neill redirected its focus to a valuable "what" that inspired his workforce to achieve on all levels. As one company manager remarked, "Paul came in and got us to do things we never thought we could do."

As Paul O'Neill's record at Alcoa so dramatically demonstrates, the most valuable "whats" of a business aren't always obvious. Over the last five years, my colleagues and I have talked with or gathered information from executives at more than 250 companies. Few of them had a serious, in-depth understanding of the contribution individual "whats" were making to overall performance. They knew the number of employee hours it took to produce their products and services, and they knew sales figures almost to the penny. Yet, when we asked which "whats" were most valuable—that is, which ones really drove business performance—many of those we interviewed couldn't answer in any significant detail.

The leaders of the companies I have worked with no longer see their organizations as collections of tasks so complex that it is impossible to identify the impact of any particular activity on business results. When they rethink, they can see what truly drives business performance.

Consider McDonald's. A look at the fast-food giant's value-generating "whats" makes it clear that it's not in the restaurant business; it's in the real estate business. McDonald's buys the land on which each of its restaurants sits, often an entire block, before it puts up a building. Then, for a fee, it turns the operations over to franchisees. Frequently, the initial franchisee can't make a go of the business and thus will be replaced by a second, third, and sometimes more franchisees. It may take years before a restaurant becomes a success, at which point the value of the property increases, and McDonald's chalks up another win. That approach carries very low risk as long as the company maintains enough basic operating volume overall.

Meanwhile, the remaining space on the block not taken up by the restaurant is leased to other businesses by the company's real estate unit. Aside from its sizeable contribution to earnings, this additional "what" makes McDonald's the largest commercial-leasing company in the world.

NEWMAN'S OWN, WHERE MORE THAN FOOD HAS VALUE

You don't have to be a corporate giant like Alcoa or McDonald's to identify your organization's most valuable "whats." Consider the much smaller Newman's Own, a privately owned company brought to life by the late, great actor Paul Newman.

In December 1980, in the basement of a red-shingled colonial in Westport, Connecticut, two men stood around a washtub stirring their homemade salad dressing with a canoe paddle. Such was the start of a business enterprise that has muscled its products onto supermarket shelves all over the United States, ringing up annual sales of more than $120 million as of 2007. Two more unlikely facts about this upstart: It is a for-profit venture that turns every cent of its earnings over to charity; and it has only 19 people on its payroll.

What Paul Newman and his buddy A.E. Hotchner were up to that December day was a simple holiday project. Newman had recently begun making his own salad dressing because he was unhappy with the taste of commercial brands—and even more unhappy about the chemical preservatives and other additives they contained. He and Hotchner, a writer by trade, were mixing a big batch of the dressing that they planned to pour into wine bottles and hand out on Christmas Eve as they and their families went caroling.

When the men finished stirring their concoction, they discovered they had made much too much. No problem, Newman decided. They would pour the excess into bottles and sell them to local food stores. To everyone's surprise, the dressing was a commercial success. The stores wanted more.

Suddenly, the hobbyists were in business, though neither partner had the slightest need to make more money. Newman was a multimillionaire from movie acting and directing, and Hotchner had a lucrative publishing career. But the real complications set in when they were advised that the dressing would be a success if, and only if, the label displayed Newman's famous name and face.

The fledgling entrepreneurs called a halt and began rethinking their enterprise. To promote his celebrity "just to line our pockets," Newman said, would be too exploitative. The only excuse for taking that low road would be if it led to a high road—say, if they gave all their profits to charity. And that is how Newman's Own became a new kind of business, one that is hugely profitable but focuses on its truly valuable "what" —namely, its ability to identify and contribute to worthy causes.

Timing also helped. America was on the cusp of the natural foods craze in 1982 when Newman's Own was founded. Devoted to products made with healthy and natural ingredients, it grew right along with Whole Foods Markets and other like-minded food purveyors. But despite all the ways in which Newman's Own is different, it has experienced most of the rites of passage of any start-up, including embarrassing pratfalls and sudden moments of enlightenment.

Early on, for example, Newman and Hotchner sought advice from a prominent marketing firm about launching their product. In-depth consumer research would cost them more than $300,000, they learned, and a proper launch program that included advertising and distribution. No thanks, said the partners; they would do it themselves. With Newman putting up $40,000 and Hotchner doing most of the work, the pair came up with their own marketing program.

But that wasn't the only unorthodox aspect of their rethinking: As much as possible, though, they wanted to outsource the "whats" of everything from manufacturing to distribution. Why? Because they didn't really care about the "whats" that were most valuable to traditional food companies; they cared about the "whats" that were most valuable to a philanthropic organization. Their big-picture outcomes revolved solely around making money just so they could give it away. In their version of plug-and-play management, then, the company's "whats" were plugged into an extension cord of sorts that connected them to vendors' operations. To this day, there is a sign over the company's office door that reads: "There are three rules you need to follow to succeed in business. Fortunately we don't know any of them."

Finding a bottler was one of the start-up's first big challenges. Large bottlers were looking for products with runs of 100,000 units or more, and celebrity-backed items were frowned upon because they generally bombed. Hotchner finally convinced a bottler outside Boston to turn the salad-dressing formula over to his chemists only to encounter yet another problem: The formula lacked the chemicals needed to assure it a decent enough shelf life. But there was a solution: Mixing the ingredients in the salad dressing would form a natural preservative gum. So the bottler whipped up his first batch of dressing—only to have the partners send it right back. Needs more work, they said, over and over again during the following six months until the bottler finally lost patience and quit.

Disheartened, but not yet ready to put a cork in their dressing idea, Newman and Hotchner arranged for a competitive tasting to see if their dressing was really better than existing brands. The event took place in the kitchen of a nearby caterer by the name of Martha Stewart (yes, that Martha Stewart) who was on her way up in the world. "If we scored poorly," the dressing duo admitted later, "we'd probably give up the ghost." But their concoction was the overwhelming favorite, and they decided to push on.

A chance encounter led to a meeting with Stew Leonard, the owner of a popular local supermarket. After having the dressing tested (it passed muster, of course), Leonard convinced the Boston bottler to reboard the Newman's Own bandwagon. It helped that the grocer was one of the bottler's largest customers and planned to order 2,000 cases of Newman's Own for his Connecticut store.

With their **Manufacture-Product** "what" in place at last, and with Leonard providing a running start for their **Distribute-Product** and **Sell-Product** "whats," Newman and Hotchner focused on their **Generate-Demand** "what." They were determined to have some fun with it by infusing a sense of humor, sort of a Newmanesque wink, into the brand along with all the good taste, healthy ingredients, and charitable works.

The playfulness in their rethought business was first apparent in their slogans, "Shameless exploitation in pursuit of the common good" and "Fine foods since February." The mock-heroic tone of the labels was accented with a kind of Napoleonic initial "N" typeface and a laurel wreath. The tongue-in-cheek slogans and labels are found on Newman's Own products to this day. The actor's image varies with the product; Newman is pictured wearing a sombrero and mustache on the salsa jar, for example, and with a set of steer horns on the steak sauce bottle.

On Newmans.com, the partners star in a goofy, silent-movie-style slide-show history of the business. Viewers learn that extra islands are what make the company's Two Thousand Island dressing better than the old standby, Thousand Island. The principals also poke fun at themselves in explaining their success: "A lot of the time we thought we were in first gear we were really in reverse, but it didn't seem to make much difference."

All kidding aside, someone has been making some good decisions about the rethought company's value-generating "whats" and the "hows" that accompany them. Its **Create-New-Product** "what," for example, is highly advanced to judge by the dozens of food items, including popcorn and fruit drinks, that now accompany the original salad dressing. Most new products still have to pass a rigorous taste test before they reach supermarket shelves. A thumbs-down verdict reached in the Westport headquarters' kitchen has held up some items as long as two years, thus derailing products that are not yet ready for prime time and might sully the brand's image.

The company has also mastered the **Identify-and-Manage-Key-Suppliers** "what." In an industry where quality control is crucial, Newman's Own vendors consistently deliver goods that live up to the company's health and taste standards. During the pet-food scare of 2007, for example, when many products manufactured abroad were recalled, the Newman brand was worry-free because it is made in the United States. (Remember the outbreak of E. coli bacteria that hammered Odwalla, the natural juice maker, in 1996? A lapse in its **Verify-Product-Quality** "what" in the manufacture of apple juice led to 49 cases of illness and the death of a small child. Overnight, the company lost a third of its market value.)

The "whats" that receive the most attention at Newman's Own, though, relate to their focus on charitable giving. Most of the 19 employees spend their time identifying the hundreds of charities that will receive a share of the company's profits, every dollar of which goes into the Newman's Own Foundation. Giving away money is getting both tougher and easier. With profits rising at a steady 10 percent a year, it's more difficult because more choices have to be made and less difficult because there is more money to fund good causes.

A major benefactor has been Hole in the Wall Camps, where children with cancer and other life-threatening diseases can spend the summer free of charge. Paul Newman established the first camp in 1988, and a total of eight now serve 18,000 kids. The camps are named after a gang whose members included Butch Cassidy and the Sundance Kid, the Wild West outlaws played by Newman and Robert Redford in the 1969 movie of the same name.

Aside from its crucial importance to the company's founders, the "whats" of **Select-Charity** and **Identify-Charity-Recipient** are also critical to the company's customers. "The younger generation doesn't buy the stuff because of me," Newman once told

The New York Times. "They don't even know me. I think they buy it because of the charity."

As the Newman's Own tale suggests, the range of possibilities for the organization of your high-value "whats" is close to infinite. Of course, chances are slim that your rethought company is going to want to outsource all of its "whats" and turn over all the profits to charity. But the use of outside vendors for "whats" that are less important, or that you lack the resources to nurture properly, is always an important option. In a global economy, no company can afford to cling to that old point of pride, "we do everything in-house."

HOW TO RETHINK YOUR "WHATS"

To identify a high-value "what," look for the answers to three basic questions:

1. Does it directly correlate with any of your company's key business goals? I find it helpful to use a scale of 1 to 5, where 1 is low or no correlation, and 5 is high correlation; the numerical quantities come in handy when reviewing and prioritizing several areas of work. Of course, you can also simply vote the "what" up or down as to its value. Here are some examples:

- Back to Alcoa for a moment, when Paul O'Neill made zero-worker-injuries the number-one goal of the organization, which required an understanding of which "whats" had the greatest influence on that, which would be a different set of "whats" than if something like profit were the top goal.

- **Resolve-Customer-Question/ Problem**. This is a "what" that exists in almost every organization. For the many automobile manufacturers that include extensive "bumper-to-bumper" warranties, this "what" can directly affect financial performance if the cost of resolving customer issues rises. But for banks or cable-television operators, let's say, it might not matter much how quickly customer complaints or questions are resolved. (And many of us have experienced that attitude, to our chagrin.) The seemingly lackadaisical attitude might stem from the fact that heavy investment to improve this "what" probably wouldn't pay off in terms of improved overall performance for either a bank or a cable-TV company.

- **Connect-to-Internet**. Wireless Internet is available in many coffee shops and other establishments today, but assessing the value of the **Connect-to-Internet** "what" can be tricky if it is viewed as a marketing "what" designed to keep customers in the store, thus making it a cost. However, if the establishment decides to charge for it, it could be a revenue-generating service. There is no right or wrong decision in this case. The key is to be specific about the role of every "what." If it's a cost instead of a source of revenue, though, then it becomes a candidate for cutting when times get lean. The message is that your treatment of your "whats" depends on their job within your organization.

2. Does it have a strong connection to your company's brand or corporate identity? Is it one of the reasons why customers feel comfortable with your brand or why your employees and partners might decide to work with you?

For retail organizations, the **Process-Returned-Merchandise** "what" is absolutely mandatory. Apparel retailer Nordstrom decided to make this "what" one of its hallmarks. Customers know that no matter what condition the product is in, no matter whether they have a receipt, or no matter if it's 20 years old, Nordstrom will take it back, no questions asked. Thinking of this high-value "what" as an aspect of marketing makes the additional cost of taking back some things other stores would not take back a tiny cost, especially when they don't spend any time or money evaluating whether the merchandise should be returned.

3. Is an effort to increase the performance of the "what" likely to cause it to become high(er) value?

   Domino's Pizza took the "whats" of **Prepare-Product**, and **Deliver-Product**, and by increasing the performance (and predictability) of the **Fulfill-Order** "what" they are both a part of, by guaranteeing home delivery of your personalized pizza in 30 minutes or less, made basic "whats" high value, brand-defining "whats"—at very low cost.

After you've rethought your enterprise and completed your search for high-value "whats," another series of questions arises: If a given "what" passes muster, how is it performing today? Why is it performing at that level? How can you enhance its performance? Should you?

If the "what" in question does not generate value, how can you trim its associated costs? Would automation or outsourcing do the job? Does the "what" duplicate work done elsewhere in the company, in which case it might be eliminated?

These are some of the issues raised in the chapter that follows.

FOUR

Second—Know What You Are (and Aren't) Good At

> *"Where I was born and where and how*
> *I have lived is unimportant.*
> *It is what I have done with where I*
> *have been that should be of interest."*
>
> *–Georgia O'Keeffe*

MICHAEL JORDAN IS ONE of the best basketball players in the history of the game. No argument. But back in 1994, he made a serious mistake. He assumed he could be one of the best at another sport as well.

Jordan was a natural athlete who could roll a bowling strike backward from between his legs, score well in pro-amateur golf tournaments, and smash batting-practice baseballs out of the park. When he announced that he was going to try his hand at professional baseball, few skeptics were bold enough to suggest that this career turn would be anything but another Jordanesque dazzler.

Jordan had led the National Basketball Association (NBA) in scoring for seven consecutive years, sparked the U.S. Olympic team to a gold medal in 1992, and led the Chicago Bulls to three straight national championships before deciding he had enough and was ready to retire from basketball. He told sportswriters that his late father had actually wanted him to be a major league baseball player. In fact, Jordan said, his greatest accomplishment in sports was being named most valuable player on his boyhood Babe Ruth League team when it won the state championship: "I batted over .500, hit five home runs in seven games, and pitched a one-hitter to get us into the championship game."

But that was then. Now, at 31, Jordan was no kid, and he faced a steep learning curve. After an underwhelming spring training season with the White Sox in 1994, he was sent to the minors. That summer he batted a modest .202 with the Class AA Birmingham Barons. His average rose to .250 with the Scottsdale Scorpions in the Arizona Fall League, but Jordan clearly was not headed for baseball stardom. The following year, he entered an ego-restoration program by rejoining the Bulls and leading them to three more NBA championships.

Some critics saw Jordan's baseball humiliation as a simple matter of hubris run wild. Viewed through a "what" lens, though, it takes on an extra dimension. Jordan assumed his high-performing "what" was **Play-Sports** when, in reality, it was simply (albeit phenomenally) **Play-Basketball**. Both his basketball and baseball "whats" could be measured by clear performance statistics—scoring and assist averages for one, batting average for the other.

For business leaders tackling the second step of the rethinking work, the task of measuring the performance of their "whats" is, as you might expect, a bit more complicated. So far in your journey toward plug-and-play management, you have learned how to identify the full range of your company's "whats" and determine which generate value and which don't. In this chapter, the focus is on their performance. You need to discover which "whats" operate at peak levels and, if not, what you should do about it.

TARGET, WHERE THE SUPPLY CHAIN "WHATS" ARE KING

One company that has mastered those skills is Target, the Minneapolis-based upscale discounter with 1,600 outlets to its name. It is constantly rethinking and adjusting its key "whats" to improve its performance, and finding ways to make the most of them to gain extra competitive advantage.

From the start, Target sought to distance itself from Wal-Mart and other discount stores whose claim to customer loyalty is low prices. Instead of plain pipe racks, Target's store displays were attractive and customer-friendly. Instead of run-of-the-million goods, Target honed its **Manage-Supply-Chain** "what" to attract top-rank designers like Isaac Mizrahi and Michael Graves to create special clothing and furnishings lines. Everything about the brand was calculated to pull in younger, better-educated, and more affluent customers—and it worked.

In 2004, Target extended its charm to Dayton Commercial Interiors, which specializes in the design and furnishing of corporate offices, hotels, hospitals, and sports venues. The 50-year-old company became a wholly owned subsidiary, and the "Dayton" in its name became "Target," a shift with special resonance since both companies once were divisions of the Dayton Hudson Department Store chain. Target Commercial Interiors (TCI) pursued business customers instead of individual consumers, but its business model and slogan—"Expect more, pay less"—were the same as its parent's, and so were its performance measures. Even though TCI's business looked very different from Target's on the surface, the newest member of the clan was expected to hew to family traditions. That meant providing extraordinary corporate design services at less-than-ordinary prices. TCI did not disappoint on either front.

In Phoenix, not far from the Scottsdale site of Michael Jordan's last baseball hurrah, TCI agreed to redecorate the interior of the Arizona Diamondbacks' stadium. It was a huge, demanding assignment, but after the work was completed, Jeffrey Moorad, the Diamondbacks' CEO, rendered his verdict: "I don't know what I like better, the job they did or what they charged us."

TCI is getting a lot of big, challenging jobs these days, in part because it has inherited Target's skill in measuring and upgrading its **Manage-Supply-Chain** "what." Imitating its parent, TCI constantly pursues the latest high-style furniture and then manages to sell it at reasonable prices. The subsidiary is also a chip off the old block in terms of the loving attention it gives to the "what" of **Manage-Brand**. "With the Target name, the world is your oyster," Joe Perdew, TCI president, told *The Wall Street Journal*.

Having a famous parent is a head start in life, but it only carries you so far. To an important degree, TCI prospers because it has identified its **Manage-Supply-Chain** "what" as a major value generator and worked hard to keep its performance level high. Knowing how well your "whats" perform is a key step on the road to plug-and-play success.

BURGERVILLE, WHERE THE FLAVOR GOES IN AND THE GARBAGE STAYS PUT

Imagine yourself wheeling into a burger joint in Vancouver, Washington. You peruse a menu that includes a Tillamook cheeseburger, made of ranch-raised beef from nearby Antelope, Oregon, and topped with a famously tasty sharp cheese made just down the road at the farmer-owned Tillamook Creamery Association. Both the meat and the cheese are hormone- and antibiotic-free. The bun is made by local bakers, too, without any preservatives.

Want some sides? How about a seasonal special like Walla Walla sweet onion rings or sweet potato fries, or a Rogue River smoky blue cheese salad with cranberries, tomatoes, and apples? And for dessert, try a milkshake, the old-fashioned kind made with real ice cream churned with milk from Oregon cows.

Welcome. You're in Burgerville. That's the name of a Vancouver-based company that boasts 39 outlets in two states (compared to over 31,000 for McDonald's) and has put uncommon effort into rethinking its two main "whats"—**Source-Raw-Materials** and **Dispose-Waste**. Superior performance in the former allows Burgerville to maintain its unusual menu of fresh local foods, and mastering waste disposal lets it reduce, reuse, and recycle 85 percent of its restaurant-generated garbage, saving significant money in the process. What is more, its restaurants run on wind power.

The chain, in part, owes its success with these critical "whats" to a careful monitoring of its performance. Customer counts and gross sales are two key measures—they were up 4 percent and 11 percent, respectively, in 2006, for example. (In fact, sales of the privately held company have risen no less than 4 percent every single year since 1995.)

Several years ago, in analyzing the performance of another key "what," **Manage-Human-Resources**, Burgerville's leaders were unhappy with the scores on two metrics, employee satisfaction and employee turnover. They instituted a new program in 2006 under which all of the company's 1,600 employees who work at least 20 hours a week pay just $15 a month for health coverage, even though the tab for the company adds up to $3 million a year. Since then, employee satisfaction scores have soared and turnover rates have plummeted, greatly reducing labor costs in the **Recruit-New-Talent** "what."

Burgerville was founded back in 1961, when its major competition was from mom-and-pop operations. The first McDonald's restaurant was barely six years old and operating in far-off Illinois. But as chain restaurants began to proliferate, George Propstra, the founder, realized that Burgerville could never compete on price. He needed to rethink his business if he were to survive, and that's just what he did: Propstra determined to make the Burgerville name synonymous with the freshest, top-drawer ingredients and to emphasize his business's success in finding local suppliers who could satisfy its high standards. The success of that neighborly approach to the **Manage-Supplier** "what" could be measured in the number of customers attracted, but there was another bottom-line metric it satisfied as well: By going local, the company eliminated the need for expensive, long-distance truck deliveries (which has echoes of our dog park "how" trap example in Chapter 1, "How the 'How' Trap Is Trapping You").

Today, the company sources more than 30,000 pounds of meat a week from Country Natural Beef's family ranches, about 600,000 eggs each year from cage-free chickens at Stiebrs Farms, and hundreds of flats of strawberries and other fruits and berries from local growers. Then there are the cheeses from Tillamook and the Rogue Creamery, milk and cream from the Sunshine Dairy, breads and rolls from family-owned Franz Bakery, cucumbers (for pickles) from nearby Skagit Valley growers, and assorted other products. All of it comes from Oregon and Washington.

Interestingly enough, the prices for Burgerville's gourmet-like offerings are remarkably similar to those of the national chains and, sometimes, even less expensive. The lowest-priced item on the Burgerville menu is the small regular burger at $1.09—made, by the way, with the same Country Natural beef and served on a Franz bun. The highest priced item is North Pacific halibut fish and chips, at $5.99.

How does Burgerville do it? In addition to the money saved on food transportation, there is the sizable sum *not* spent transporting its garbage to landfills. Having found the performance of its **Dispose-Waste** "what" inadequate, the company embarked on a major sustainability program. Now 85 percent of the 340 tons of garbage the chain accumulates each month, enough to cover an area the size of a basketball court to a height of 16 feet, is being composted and recycled at a savings of at least $100,000 a year—a significant sum for an organization the size of Burgerville. (On a per restaurant comparison, McDonald's is about 800 times the size of Burgerville, so that would be about $80 million in savings for McDonald's, no small potatoes.)

Burgerville's restaurant employees put recyclable and compostable materials into color-coded containers. The organic waste is then turned into a nutrient-rich compost that can be sold to businesses and homeowners to enrich and enhance their soil. Also, Burgerville's used cooking oil—some 7,500 gallons monthly—is picked up by an outside contractor and converted into 6,400 gallons of biodiesel, a fuel that is less toxic to the environment. Right now, the arrangement saves Burgerville the cost of hauling the greasy stuff away. But, eventually, as a competitive market in renewable fuels develops, that waste oil is likely to turn into a source of revenue.

Burgerville's determined attention to waste disposal and local produce has earned Tom Mears, who took over as CEO when Propstra, his father-in-law, retired in 1992, the 2007 Trendsetter Award by the Foodservice Consultants Society International. The award was a tribute to, among other things, his smart management of his company's **Source-Raw-Materials** and **Dispose-Waste** "whats."

I should point out that although Burgerville and McDonald's share many "whats," being in the same industry and all, the way they go about those "whats"—their "hows"—are very different. So their leaders have to be careful when measuring performance against industry benchmarks or when dropping in new information technology. I have made much of the importance of forgetting about your "hows" to concentrate on your "whats," but you do need to have a clear sense of the "how" behind every "what" before you begin rethinking your organization.

AN ELECTRONICS GIANT THAT'S GOT THE JUICE

In another business and on another continent, an industrial giant you've probably never heard of has so completely rethought and mastered its **Manufacture-Product** "what" that competitors in the electronics business can only look on with envy.

Hon Hai Precision Industry is a Taiwanese company that makes many of those electronic items the world can't seem to get enough of. The logos may read Apple, Dell, HP, Nokia, Sony, and the like, but most of the phones, MP3 players, video-game players, printers, and PCs are actually made by the world's number one electronics manufacturer, Hon Hai.

The company started out in 1974 as a supplier of plastics. Then, in 1981, when personal computing was the new, new thing, Hon Hai's savvy and aggressive founder Terry Gou entered the connector business. From that beachhead, Gou has seized every opportunity to extend vertically into other electronic products as sales of older ones begin to wane. The Hon Hai juggernaut's latest extensions include LCD panels, cameras, and notebook PCs.

The statistics that describe Hon Hai are staggering. For instance, it employs 360,000 people in factories that stretch from Mexico to Malaysia, including a massive facility in China's Guangdong Province that employs 200,000. The place is so big that it has its own soccer complex, chicken farm, and police force. Sites in China, Mexico, and Eastern Europe thriftily mass produce high-volume, labor-intensive products at lower cost, while U.S. and Japanese locations provide R&D and engineering support. All the Hon Hai manufacturing facilities are linked by efficient *enterprise resource planning* (ERP) software systems.

In 2006, Hon Hai's sales surged by 44 percent, to $40 billion, besting the combined revenues of its three biggest rivals. Meanwhile, Hon Hai's profits jumped even more, rising 47 percent, to $1.8 billion. Investors took notice, sending the company's shares up by 52 percent in a 12-month period, as struggling competitors saw their stock prices plummet. And in the opinion of equity analysts at Credit Suisse and Yuanta Research, the future holds more of the same.

As with many other Taiwanese-based manufacturers, Hon Hai has honed its ability to keep costs low, turn out goods rapidly, and nimbly adjust its operations to accommodate new products. But what sets it apart from the crowd is its own finely tuned **Manufacture-Product** "what." The company has clearly identified the "whats" that are most valuable and invested the necessary resources to make sure it performs at peak efficiency.

Noted for its high-precision mechanical expertise, Hon Hai actually codevelops and makes many of the components—like circuit boards, thermal components, and iPod casings—that go into the goods it assembles for its premium OEM client base, thus shortening the cycle time of the **Develop-Product** "what." Quick turnaround is particularly important in the electronics industry, where short product life cycles and the accompanying price erosion can squeeze margins.

In an industry where the supply chain is constantly under pressure in terms of pricing and consolidation—much of it initiated by Hon Hai itself—the company presents a portrait of a manufacturing business at the top of its game. With exceptionally strong finances and manufacturing expertise—supported by a business model that is both cost- and time-efficient—Hon Hai is fast becoming a one-stop-shopping place for some of the world's most sought-after electronic brands.

HOW TO RETHINK YOUR "WHATS"

In analyzing the performance of your "whats" and planning improvements, you need to know just how much value each "what" contributes. Essentially, there are four combinations to work through.

They are listed here, with a thumbnail suggestion as to your reaction:

1. **High value/low performance:** Pay serious attention.

2. **High value/high performance:** Monitor.

3. **Low value/low performance:** Consider automating, outsourcing, or even eliminating it.

4. **Low value/high performance:** Same advice; could be a major waste of resources.

As to the actual process of judging performance, I favor using a scale of 1 to 5, with 1 being the lowest level. So, your first task is to give the "what" under consideration a numerical grade. First ask how it is currently performing. Then, I suggest you ask three further questions:

- How is it currently performing today?

- Do we know and understand what causes performance today?

- Do we know and understand what it would take to improve performance?

If the performance level is under 3, and the answer to one of the last two questions is negative, you can safely put that "what" aside for future consideration to concentrate on improving those that are high in value and low in performance.

After you pinpoint the "whats" that seem to warrant your attention, another level of questions should be asked during the thinking process—questions that can help you determine what to plug in and what to unplug. They are discussed in the next three chapters, starting, in the pages just ahead, with an exploration of the web of connections that link your company's "whats."

FIVE

Third—Make (and Break) Connections

"I was always independent,
even when I had partners."

–Samuel Goldwyn

WHEN YOU RETHINK YOUR company and study it using the "what" as your unit of analysis, you can see that, at its core, it is a tightly woven fabric of connections—emotional, financial, technical— that cut across organizational boundaries. Pull on one thread and many others might move. The clerk in accounting is related to the chief dispatcher who went to school with the director of advertising. A glitch in production or a spurt in sales can send shock waves from one end of the company to the other, from design to delivery, and it might well affect the bottom line.

So before you act upon your knowledge of which "whats" are high in value and low in performance, before you set in motion a process-improvement program, you need to examine the connections between and among your target "whats." A failure to do so can wreak havoc with a company's profits and prospects. Dell Inc. learned that lesson the hard way.

Dell was launched in 1984 by a young entrepreneur with a brilliant strategy. He would sell made-to-order computers directly to customers, primarily businesses, without benefit of retail outlets. The brick-and-mortar middlemen were charging too much, Michael Dell concluded, and giving customers ridiculously inadequate technical support to boot. He intended to sidestep both pitfalls. In particular, his company was going to provide outstanding tech support.

And it did that famously, until the day it didn't, infamously.

In the early 2000s, in pursuit of lower overhead, Dell began to outsource the resolve **Customer-Questions/Problems** "what" to a call center in India. Costs fell all right, but so did customer satisfaction. Angry callers complained about everything from their difficulties in understanding the Indian operators' accents to over-scripted responses and delays in reaching high-level technical people.

What Dell had overlooked—inexplicably, given its founder's original insight—was the strong connection its customers felt with its **Resolve-Customer-Questions/Problems** "what." Dell conditioned people to expect the best, and, suddenly, the company was delivering anything but.

Dell awoke from its slumber in 2003 and tried to repair the damage caused by the broken connection. The company announced that support calls for two of its key models, a desktop computer and a notebook, would now be routed not to India but to an existing call center in the United States. Other computer models would still be served by a call center in Bangalore, but the tech-support staff there would be increased and taught new approaches.

Some Dell agents received special training in handling complex problems, thus allowing customers to deal with only one tech representative per call.

Yet over the next few years, criticism of the **Resolve-Customer-Questions/Problems** "what" increased. Dell's ratings from Technology Business Research (TBR) showed it still leading the pack in tech support but steadily losing ground to rivals. *Consumer Reports* kept downgrading its scores.

In July 2005, Jeff Jarvis, using his influential tech blog, BuzzMachine, lit into the corporation. "I just got a new Dell laptop and paid a fortune for the four-year, in-home service," he wrote. "The machine is a lemon, and the service is a lie." Jarvis's grousing became the blogosphere's third most-linked-to post that day, inspiring hundreds more rants.

Dell responded to the firestorm by announcing a $150 million campaign to fix its **Resolve-Customer-Questions/Problems** "what," mainly by improving call-center responses. It claimed the average wait time to reach a senior technical person had been cut from nine minutes to three. By now, though, the company's problems went well beyond tech support. Dell's **Manage-Finances** and **Manufacture-Product** "whats" were under fire, too.

In January 2007, Michael Dell finally took back hands-on control of the company, returning as CEO, a position he had ceded for a few years. The repairs

ordered for the **Resolve-Customer-Questions/
Problems** "what" began to pay off, leading the company to improve its ranking in the TBR customer-
satisfaction study. Dell was generally perceived as
being in comeback mode.

But how, you may ask, could a company that built
its reputation on superlative customer service
make such a mistake? In fact, in my experience,
the failure to recognize key connections is com-
monplace. Companies are immensely complex
organisms, intrinsically difficult to comprehend
in their entirety. That's why I urge you to rethink
the linkages of every "what," no matter its value or
level of performance, before you start plugging and
playing.

Connections between "whats" can take diverse and
often unexpected forms. Interpersonal relationships, for example, might create a tightly woven,
far-from-obvious web among several "whats." Such
linkages might improve performance or impede it.
Enterprisewide software programs are, in and of
themselves, a web of connections, linking virtually
every "what" within an organization and the people
and technologies that are part of it.

Not all "whats" are created—or connected—equal,
and it's much easier to manage and move them
effectively if you understand how they connect
and how those connections affect their performance and the enterprise as a whole. If a particular

low-value "what" is not tightly interconnected, for example, it might be a good candidate for automation, outsourcing, or elimination. If a high-value "what" is tightly interconnected, like Dell's **Resolve-Customer-Questions/Problems'** relationship with customers, it might be wise to change it only slowly, if at all. By the same token, "whats" that seem tangential and better performed by a vendor might nevertheless have to be kept in-house because their disappearance would hinder the workings of the more valuable "whats" to which they closely link.

MERCK: BEYOND THE MOAT

In one of his final public appearances as chairman, president, and CEO of Merck & Company, Raymond V. Gilmartin told a Texas audience in 2005 of the "countless lives" saved by the medications his company developed over the years. It was an impressive array, ranging from penicillin and measles and mumps vaccines to Zocor, which lowers cholesterol. Gilmartin's pride in Merck's scientists and their discoveries was palpable, a reflection of the company's century-old concentration on in-house research.

But, today the "we-can-do-it-all" mandate no longer rules Merck's labs. From headquarters in suburban Whitehouse Station, New Jersey, the word has gone forth as part of the rethinking that downgraded "hows" in favor of "whats." Merck now welcomes new product ideas from scientists wherever they may be. The company is acquiring some research firms and aggressively pursuing alliances with dozens of others. As one Merck researcher put it, "We've gone from inward facing to outward looking." An astonishing one-third of the company's $24 billion in annual revenue now comes from the products and patents of its partners.

For Merck and for other members of Big Pharma that have followed the same path, this radical change has led to some heavy-duty soul-searching about their relationships to new outside partners and suppliers. Suddenly, instead of running the show, they have to share control. That means learning a new set of cooperation and communication skills. It also means building new connections between the company's existing "whats" and those of its partners and suppliers.

Drug companies' single-most pressing need is for new discoveries to fill their product pipelines. And with a generation of top-selling medications going off patent, the companies have been desperate for new blockbusters to take their place. When their own labs fail to do the job, pharmas look for promising formulations outside their walls.

Merck has 12 drug scouts working in seven countries. According to *Fast Company* magazine, they checked out 5,000 biotech companies and medical schools in 2006 alone. Their work paid off in 53 licensing deals. And over the three years from 2004 to 2007, when the "we" in "we can do it" gave way to "they," the number of licensed products in Merck's pipeline tripled from 4 to 12. An unsurprising result of rethinking.

When Raymond Gilmartin recounted Merck's medical triumphs back in 2005, one drug was notably absent from the list—Vioxx. Although the drug eased the pain of arthritis without any of the digestive problems that bedeviled its rivals, it had a much more serious negative side effect: Vioxx had been found to increase the risk of heart attack and stroke. The company pulled it from the market in 2004 after being accused of knowingly ignoring the dangers. By year-end 2005, Gilmartin had pulled out as well. Aside from the damage to its brand, Merck spent more than $1.2 billion defending itself against 27,000 Vioxx-related lawsuits; it finally agreed to pay $4.85 billion to settle those claims.

Vioxx was not Merck's only problem. Patents on two of its best-selling medications were set to expire— Zocor in 2006 and Fosamax, used to treat osteoporosis, in 2007. Nor was the company's drug pipeline anywhere near full. Merck's in-house expertise in organic chemistry, a famously complex field, had been a world-beater in its day, but now the breakthroughs were coming from biotech and vaccines, areas in which its labs did not excel.

What Merck did have was cash, and it spent lavishly to catch up. It signed dozens of licensing and codevelopment deals with outside research firms, learning an important lesson in connectivity along the way: how to align its "whats" with those of another research organization.

In 2006, for example, the company reached an agreement with Boston-based Paratek Pharmaceuticals to develop and market MK-2764, a new class of antibiotic that shows promise of coping with the rash of drug-resistant infections. Thomas J. Bigger, Paratek's president and CEO, offered a frank assessment of his giant new partner: "Its embrace of the collaborative process demonstrates a new side of Merck that we found very compelling."

The big connectivity challenge for Merck and the other big pharmaceuticals, as noted earlier, is control, and it's not simply a matter of ego. Because they are uniquely subject to regulatory oversight and class-action lawsuits, they feel the need to keep an eye on every step of a drug's development. Yet, it's a fine line to walk, because no independent lab wants to be constantly second-guessed by a team of Big Pharma researchers, and such interference can have a seriously negative impact on the research.

Essentially, pharmaceutical companies like Merck
have rethought their activities and investigated how
their strong in-house "whats" would connect with
the strong inside "whats" of an outside collaborator.
They then defined their goals and established the
price they are willing to pay to achieve them.

For any organization, yours included, that balance between goals and price needs to be clear and
firm. A 2007 survey found that pharmas are sometimes inconsistent when contracting with outside
interests—a previous emphasis on innovation, for
example, might yield to dollar concerns. Too often,
important aspects of the connection between
in-house and outside "whats" are ignored until
a disagreement arises. Lacking an agreed-upon
framework, tempers tend to overheat and mountains rise from molehills. Clear benchmarks of
progress and dispute-resolution procedures should
be set forth in the original agreement. In the case of
the pharmaceuticals, it should spell out, for example, the circumstances under which a scientific
quarrel between pharma and lab personnel would
be referred to upper management.

The successful management of "whats" that cross
organizational boundaries requires special training. Yet, the 2007 survey discovered that six out
of ten respondents with outsourcing responsibili-
ties had only on-the-job experience and no for-
mal training. For pharmaceutical companies, in

particular, connectivity management touches on delicate emotional issues that need to be considered. The failure of the company research labs to live up to the we-can-do-it-all mantra of the past is one element; the reduction in research jobs due to outsourcing is another. And where is it written that technical people are necessarily adept at communication and collaboration?

In terms of managing connections across its "whats," Merck seems to be ahead of the game. At a conference in 2007, Richard T. Clark, Gilmartin's successor as chairman, president, and CEO, boasted about how much faster Merck is now moving drugs through R&D. Using Six Sigma-speak, he credited the improvement in part to the "black belts working along with physicians and clinicians in research," describing them as "experts in how to deal with supply chains." The lesson for other organizations is this: Until you train or hire such experts, you will have trouble making the most of your "whats" in any kind of outsourcing arrangement.

Whether the decision to be made concerns outsourcing, acquisitions, increased investment in a particular "what," technology initiatives like Software Plus Services (S+S), or some other aspect of corporate life, connectivity issues have to be addressed. They can literally determine the success or failure of any project.

HOW TO RETHINK YOUR "WHATS"

When considering a plug-and-play approach with any given "what," you need to get a fix on its interconnectedness. Is it intimately, somewhat, or lightly involved with other in-house "whats," or with the "whats" of partners, suppliers, regulators, or even customers?

If the "what" you've targeted for improvement or automation is highly interconnected, that extra complexity is likely to add to the project's cost and risk. The **Manufacture-Product** "what," for example, requires a large number of inputs from various sources, and its outputs go in many directions. All those human and mechanical connections need to be factored into the improvement or automation equation. Will the change you have in mind increase costs for a supplier of raw materials or require a major revision of your product warranty? Will it rupture your relationship with a longtime partner? In other words, will the change be worth all the attendant hassle? By the same token, such a highly connected "what," even if it has been previously defined as low-value and low-performing, might be difficult to outsource because it breaks virtually all the relationships that have been built up over the years.

On the other hand, a "what" such as **Pay-Employees** has a low level of connectedness to other "whats." It's an important activity, of course, but it doesn't, in and of itself, contribute high value as defined in Chapter 3, "First—Identify the 'Whats' That Are Truly Valuable." So if you plan to improve its operation, there will be relatively few complications because of links to other "whats." In fact, its limited connectedness and low value make it a popular candidate for outsourcing.

Don't underestimate the importance of the personal factor. If there are family ties between the head of payroll and a high-level executive, any move to outsource the pay-employees "what" is likely to encounter static. And you are going to think twice about any improvement plan that would negatively affect a supplier whose CEO is best friends with your major customer.

Note that the many caveats I have included in this chapter are not intended to disparage the ties that bind a company together. Interconnectedness is a powerful and necessary aspect of a successful organization. Often, though, these relationships are ignored when companies set about making operational improvements. Leaders become so intent on the immediate details of a job, the "hows," that they overlook the connections as well as the "whats." That can lead to disaster.

As I wrote this book, I thought of myself as a kind of
optometrist working to find just the right combination of lenses that would give your company a clear,
well-focused view of the world. In each chapter, I
tried to add another lens. In the pages just ahead,
the view is expanded by the predictability of your
"whats."

SIX

Fourth—Understand What Can (and Can't) Be Predicted

> "I don't try to describe the future. I try to prevent it."
>
> –Ray Bradbury

IN THE COURSE OF RETHINKING, you have learned how to identify your "whats," determine their value and performance level, and figure out their connections to one another. The next step is to train the lens of predictability on your stakeholders—customers, suppliers, and partners—to anticipate their responses to the plug-and-play changes you want to make.

One of the more dramatic—and potentially traumatic—examples of "what" unpredictability occurred some years ago, when Chrysler decided to examine the vendors supplying parts for its Jeep Cherokee. The analysis of the company's **Manufacture-Product** "what" started with the V-8 engine assembled by Chrysler, focusing first on the roller-lifter valve. The valve was manufactured by Eaton, which, in turn, contracted with a neighboring factory to provide unfinished metal castings. That factory, it turned out, relied on yet another supplier for the special clay used in making the castings.

When the Chrysler team contacted the owner of the clay company, he dropped a bad-news bombshell. Selling clay to the castings maker was a losing proposition, he told them, so he was switching into a new business—kitty litter. Had he mentioned his plans to Chrysler's castings supplier? Uh, no.

Suppose Chrysler had never surveyed its Jeep Cherokee **Manufacture-Product** "what." A for-want-of-a-nail scenario could have played out: no clay, no castings, no roller-lifter valve, no V-8 engine, no Jeep Cherokee.

Predicting how a "what" will behave under a new set of circumstances can be as difficult as it is essential. A case in point: the Boeing 787 Dreamliner.

Back in 2002, Boeing made a momentous decision. To produce its revolutionary Dreamliner in record time, the company's **Manufacture-Product** "whats" would be rearranged. The plan called for major subcontractors to share the new plane's development costs while building large sections free of Boeing micromanagement. Finished parts would be flown to Boeing's assembly plant in Everett, Washington, and snapped together in as little as three days. Boeing would save billions of dollars.

Fly forward five years to July 8, 2007. The first production model of the Dreamliner was unveiled at Everett. Some 15,000 invited guests, the cream of the aerospace industry, listened respectfully as former NBC news anchor Tom Brokaw emceed the ceremony and broadcasters relayed it via satellite to 45 countries in nine languages.

So much jubilation for so little reality. Under its shiny coat, the 787 was, in fact, a Potemkin jetliner. Because of an industrywide shortage of the fasteners needed to assemble its parts, it had been juryrigged with temporary ones that had to be popped out and replaced after the ceremony. Large sections of the plane arrived without proper documentation from the subcontractors. Much of its wiring had yet to be installed, and its flight control software, with more than 6 million lines of code, had not been delivered by Honeywell.

Teams of Boeing troubleshooters had been on the road for a year, visiting subcontractors. Even so, unexpected problems cropped up everywhere. The new carbon composite skin was a nightmare. For the wing sections and huge fuselage barrels, 19 feet in diameter and 22 feet long, enormous ribbons of carbon fiber soaked in a mixture of polymers had to be plastered into molds or carefully wound onto cylinders and baked in a giant oven, maintaining uniform thickness and avoiding blistering problems that could endanger the airplane. The Japanese supplier of the composite materials, Toray Industries, had no experience with large-scale production. The contractors in Italy, Japan, and South Carolina that were charged with fabricating the stuff into wings and fuselage barrels had no experience working with the materials, either. Other suppliers had trouble maintaining quality and staying within budget—not to mention the excess weight that threatened the Dreamliner's promised economy.

I'll get back to the Boeing saga shortly, but first, a few general observations. *Predictability* is one of the most treasured business qualities. Uncertainty is anathema because it's risky, and I suspect that you, like most businesspeople, are not a gambler. (Or to be a bit more precise, it doesn't make sense to gamble when you don't know the odds.) So in the course of rethinking, the ability to predict how your key "whats" will behave under different circumstances becomes critical to your planning.

To be sure, as you plug and play your "whats," not every twist and turn can be predicted with ironclad certainty. That's unrealistic. But you can become much more aware of the possible reactions, good and bad, of various "whats" as they undergo change, removal, or automation. Beyond that, there is enormous value in knowing what you cannot predict. Just like knowing the odds in gambling, understanding what you are getting into and the predictability of the outcome can inform your appetite for that risk/gamble.

Generally speaking, the greater complexity of the "what" (intricacy adds variation), the more unpredictability and longer timeframe. So the manufacture of a jetliner encompasses the worst of both worlds; it is hugely complicated and takes years to complete.

Boeing might have started with every intention of predicting where newly outsourced Dreamliner "whats" might stumble, but no evidence of that exists. In fact, apparently there was a widespread assumption that all would go well, given that no contingency plans were prepared in case the revolutionary rearrangement of the **Manufacture-Product** "whats" malfunctioned.

From the beginning, Boeing's leaders knew the 787 was a huge gamble. It was also, however, a necessity. As the new century began, Boeing was in a tailspin. Struggling to digest three major acquisitions, the company had allowed its European rival, Airbus, to take the lead in total jetliner sales and to continue to build its market share. While Boeing hunkered down, failing to come up with new models and suffering production setbacks, Airbus was stealing the spotlight by announcing its giant A380, a 550-passenger colossus that instantly captured the world's attention and built a backlog of orders.

Boeing decided against trying to match the A380, which it considered too big and too likely to perpetuate the airline industry's hated hub-and-spoke route structure. Instead, the company opted to build a supersonic plane that could bypass hub airports by flying longer distances nonstop. But the airlines were lukewarm. More airspeed would still leave passengers fighting slow ground traffic in airports and on highways. Eventually, Boeing recognized that what the airlines really wanted was more efficiency, meaning a comfortable jetliner that pleased passengers and cost far less to operate.

That's how Boeing came to launch the 7E7 program—"E" for efficiency—which became the

787 Dreamliner. Boeing engineers used composite materials for parts that eventually made up 50 percent of the plane's weight, more than doubling the 20 percent composite total in the earlier 777. This engineering feat made it possible to reap substantial savings on fuel and increased efficiency.

In addition, Boeing outsourced an astonishing 70 percent of the actual manufacturing "whats," up from 50 percent for the 777, thus distributing both greater risk and greater autonomy to its suppliers. For businesses like Newman's Own, discussed in Chapter 3, "First—Identify the 'Whats' That Are Truly Valuable," whose products are not terribly complex and their goals unorthodox (making money to give it away), wholesale outsourcing makes great sense. But for a product that is as complex as an airplane, where lives are literally at risk every time the plane leaves the ground, outsourcing so many "whats" is a much riskier way to eliminate those pesky "hows."

Amid all the innovation, few people grasped until later that no one at Boeing had predicted how the company's various manufacturing "whats" would behave in the hands of suppliers.

At first, events favored Boeing. Airbus ran into repeated problems with its A380, which fell two years behind schedule. Meanwhile, airlines were attracted to the lightweight, efficient Dreamliner—

and all the more so when the price of jet fuel began to soar. Airbus tried to compete by introducing a new plane, the extra-wide-body A350, but its aluminum skin was no match for the Dreamliner's composite material. By mid-2007, some 47 customers had placed orders for a total of 677 Dreamliners. Just before the 787's unveiling, Boeing CFO James Bell hailed it as "the most successful launch in the history of civil aviation." New buyers would have to wait for delivery until at least 2012, though. "We're sold out," Bell said, adding that no speedup could occur "until we see what kind of capacity we have in the production chain."

In reality, the situation with the plane's manufacturing "whats" was already all too plain. The 787's first flight test had been postponed from August to mid-November. Undaunted, Boeing insisted that the first delivery would still be made to All Nippon Airways as promised in May of 2008. The schedule allowed only 5 months for flight testing and certification, compared to the 11 months it took for the 777 to pass muster. In mid-October, Boeing finally admitted that the first 787 delivery would not occur until late November or early December of 2008. Boeing stock dropped; airline customers seethed. Chinese airline executives, who had been counting on the Dreamliner to fly visitors to the 2008 Olympic Games starting in August, were especially incensed.

Boeing's leaders minimized the problem, calling it nothing more than "growing pains at the front end" of the program. By way of example, they explained how subcontractors Alenia Aeronautica of Italy and Vought Aircraft of Dallas, which built a factory in Charleston, South Carolina, to fabricate some of the 787 fuselage barrels, had hired inexperienced local workers to build the most technically advanced commercial airplane in history. After the fact, it didn't take a genius to predict trouble or to have a contingency plan ready in case those particular "whats" unraveled.

The larger lesson: Before you embark on a rethinking initiative to alter your "whats," especially those that generate substantial value for your company, you'd better have a clear sense of what the effects will be. Those predictions should help you decide whether to pursue the changes or, if you do go ahead, how to prepare for any negative impact.

JETBLUE: STORM WARNINGS

Valentine's Day 2007 dawned cold and wet, with the East Coast enveloped in Mother Nature's icy grip. Early that morning, JetBlue Airways loaded passengers onto six flights at New York's John F. Kennedy Airport, holding them on runways ready to take off as soon as the expected break in the weather arrived. The break never came. Meanwhile, other planes were waiting at the gates, and new ones were arriving all the time.

The result was gridlock. Passengers were trapped on planes for up to eight hours as food and water gave out and toilets overflowed. Inside JFK's terminals, it was no picnic, either. Would-be passengers spent days waiting for a chance to fly home, sleeping on floors and subsisting on snack foods and airport fare.

Charles Mees, JetBlue's chief information officer, had been relaxing at company headquarters not far from the airport when the first damage reports came in. He and his team of 80 IT people rushed to JFK. Over the next three days, Mees cleaned aircraft, worked the baggage claim area, manned the ticket counters and gates, and desperately tried to bring order out of chaos—all this on only an hour or two of sleep each night. But his heroics did not shield Mees from passenger wrath. On the evening of February 16, for instance, he had to tell thousands of people waiting in the airport lobby that JetBlue was shutting down for the night. "Don't come back tomorrow," he added, "because all those flights are full, as are all the flights on Sunday and probably Monday, too." The response? "I heard some pretty colorful language," he told *CIO* magazine.

In the crunch triggered by the Valentine's Day calamity, virtually every "what" the airline had in place self-destructed, including the following:

- **Create-Passenger-Reservation**

- **Issue-Passenger-Ticket**

- **Collect-Passenger-Baggage**

- **Schedule-Ground-Crew**

- **Schedule-Flight-Crew**

And so on. It was a total systems meltdown. How was it possible, you might ask, that a company as smart and successful as JetBlue could fall apart so completely while its competitors were weathering the storm? The answer, in brief: The company's leaders had failed to adequately predict how the company's various "whats" would perform in extreme conditions. Need I add that you don't have to be an airline to suffer dire consequences if you're not aware of the risks associated with your "whats."

When JetBlue was founded in 2001, in defiance of prevailing industry wisdom, its leaders promised passengers a seemingly impossible combination of great customer service at cut-rate fares. They delivered, too. Passenger miles and new destinations skyrocketed, so that, by the fall of 2006, JetBlue was handling more than 500 flights a day to 53 cities. That year, revenues reached $2.4 billion. Then came the Valentine's Day breakdown.

The media pegged it as a man-bites-dog news story—a high-flying enterprise brought down. The ubiquity of cell phones helped to keep the story on the front page for days, as all sorts of first-person accounts and graphic photographs of enraged passengers, stranded aircraft, and mountains of lost luggage poured out onto the 24-hour news channels and the blogosphere.

The company issued endless apologies, and then-CEO David Neeleman spent a week repeating the mantra-like phrase, "Words cannot express how truly sorry we are," on television and radio shows, including *Today* and in interviews with David Letterman and Anderson Cooper. He announced a "Customer Bill of Rights," which included various levels of reimbursement for JetBlue passengers, depending on how long their flights had been delayed. By month's end, ticket sales were back to normal.

Nevertheless, the shockingly poor performance led to Neeleman's departure as CEO (he's now JetBlue's chairman), and it cost the company tens of millions of dollars. The blunders also deflated outsized opinions about JetBlue. No one who was there or who read about the systems' collapse or heard from the airline's passengers during those horrendous days is likely to forget it. Low fares will always be a draw, but for many who had deeply admired JetBlue, the honeymoon was over.

What made the meltdown all the more frustrating for many insiders was this: There had been earlier signs that the airline was in trouble. Rapid growth had begun to take its toll on operational efficiency back in 2005, when the airline posted the first of what would be back-to-back annual net losses. Someone should have seized the controls and stopped the downward spiral, but it just didn't happen. Instead, risks were ignored or overlooked. You can understand how that happens—when trouble arrives, the cry is for instant fixes, not for a patient exploration of the potential dangers attached to your company's "whats."

The moral: Get your risk assessment before the sky falls in.

JetBlue's problem "whats" included the following:

- **Schedule-Flight:** From the start, JetBlue had a built-in prejudice against canceling flights. It was part of the company culture and strongly supported by Neeleman. As a start-up, the airline got away with occasionally holding passengers on aircraft for long periods of time. However, if the organization's leaders had bothered to predict how this "what" would respond as the airline grew and began carrying thousands of passengers daily, they would have seen the need for a contingency plan. Rival airlines had canceled flights and avoided a Valentine's Day fiasco. Having learned its lesson, JetBlue now cancels many more flights when the weather is, or is about to become, foul.

- **Schedule-Flight-Crew:** Even when planes became available for takeoff during the February storms, the company had trouble locating crews to man them. Because FAA rules limit the number of hours crew members can work, those on duty had to be replaced as airport delays mounted. The electronic systems for locating and contacting replacements for this vital "what" were slow and untested under crisis conditions. When the test came, they flunked. Since then, vendors have removed glitches, and JetBlue has developed a system that broadcasts a message to crew members' cell phones and pagers, asking them to check in.

- **Manage-Communications:** The JetBlue call center was quickly overwhelmed during the Valentine's Day massacre. No serious thought had been given to predicting how that "what" might bear up in such a crisis, nor had alternatives

been considered. In the aftermath, the
company decided to upgrade JetBlue.
com to enable customers to do more for
themselves.

I offer the story of JetBlue's 2007 troubles as a
cautionary tale. You can't read it, I hope, without
thinking about your own company and the degree
to which it has achieved an intimate knowledge of
its key "whats" and the risks attending them. It's not
enough to manage an enterprise for today, or even
tomorrow. Leaders who fail to predict and prepare
for worst-case scenarios of their "whats" are invit-
ing disaster.

HOW TO RETHINK YOUR "WHATS"

In preparation for rethinking your organization
and successfully introducing plug-and-play management, you need to determine how predictable
your target "whats" are. How sure are you that
these "whats" will actually achieve their desired
outcomes? To the degree that you're unsure, you
need to ask why.

Is the unpredictability attached to a particular
"what" caused by some common, well-recognized
factors that you can control or easily make allow-
ance for? Or is it caused by unknown factors or
those beyond your control? If the latter, you would

be well advised to back off, at least until your understanding and control improves. The flip side of this is that when something unpredictable happens, like the emergency that leveled JetBlue, there must be specific emergency "whats" to manage the predictability of how you perform in these situations.

In handling thousands of visitors a day, Amazon. com has made the **Create-New-Customer** "what" almost completely predictable. Without any need for human direction, the site's software ushers customers through the purchase process, answering questions and solving problems. The condition of the site's technology represents the only area of unpredictability, and I assume Amazon has a contingency plan ready if needed.

Boeing, on the other hand, gambled on an unpredictable **Manufacture-Product** "what" by outsourcing such a large chunk of its Dreamliner. And it increased the risk, in some cases, by using vendors with limited experience.

To limit risk and maximize benefit, you should look first to "whats" that have high business value (so they're worth improving) and poor performance (so there's room for improvement) and high predictability (so the risk of failure is slight).

As I suggested previously, the greater your ability to control the variables in the operation of your company's "whats," the better you can predict how they will react to improvement, outsourcing, or automation. Some elements of any business, though, are virtually control-proof.

Umbrella manufacturers can do nothing about any given year's weather patterns, for instance, and clothing manufacturers are constantly blindsided by a sudden change in consumer habits or tastes. And there is one major outside phenomenon that affects every business and will be obeyed—governmental actions, rules, and regulations. The next chapter offers some advice in preparing for and coping with them.

SEVEN

Fifth—Unravel (and Follow) the Rules

"Sometimes it is more important to discover what one cannot do than what one can do."

–Lin Yutang

IN RETHINKING YOUR business to put aside "how" in favor of "what" as your unit of analysis, your view of your company has been expanded through the lenses of value, performance, interconnectedness, and predictability. Now it's time to think about government regulation. That is not to suggest that the laws and rules set forth by the various branches of government are anything new; they have long loomed large in every company's business plan and daily operation. What this chapter offers are new ways to incorporate compliance needs into your planning.

The tale of Intrade, the Dublin-based, online prediction market, is instructive. For the first four years of its life, the company barreled from strength to strength. The lure was strong: Members could buy or sell futures contracts on upcoming events—anything from the outcome of an election to the likelihood of Osama Bin Laden's capture. If the price of the contract rose high enough or sank low enough, members could make a bundle.

The founder and CEO, John Delaney, didn't have to worry about promotion. Intrade's market predictions were so accurate that the media followed them closely and often. In 2004, for example, it accurately predicted the outcome of the presidential election and all but one member of the U.S. Congress. Why so accurate? According to Harvard economist N. Gregory Mankiw, "Everybody has information from their own little corner of the universe, and they'd like to know the information from every other corner of the universe. What these markets do is provide a vehicle that reflects all that information."

Intrade was something new in the world, and the world sat up and took notice. By 2006, membership had soared to 75,000, more than two-thirds of it American. The number of markets in which to invest had passed the 58,000 mark. The Trade Exchange Network, Intrade's parent company, had started negotiations to make the site a regulated exchange in the United States.

Then the roof fell in. In October of 2006, Congress passed, and President George W. Bush signed, the Unlawful Internet Gambling Enforcement Act, which had been tacked on in a midnight session to another piece of legislation involving port security. It suddenly became illegal for U.S. banks and credit card companies to transfer funds to an online gambling site.

For publicly owned Web-based gambling companies, the impact was devastating—$8 billion in market value vanished within days. Intrade, which is privately held, got hammered as well, even though its executives insist it is not a gambling site, but a market where traders rely on their predictive skills. That's not how U.S. banks saw it, however.

And with credit card charges from its site banned, Intrade's U.S. revenues plummeted by 70 percent before the month was out.

Intrade is not the first, and surely will not be the last, company to feel the sting of a sudden new action by a duly constituted government agency or legislative body. Auto manufacturers are intermittently slammed by new state or federal emission rules. Unexpected changes in labeling rules have caused havoc in the food industry, and, of course, many of us have experienced the impact of added security regulations in airports.

For people in every industry, the message should be clear: Be prepared. A thorough understanding of your company's existing or potential compliance issues is essential. And before you rethink and perhaps make major changes to one of your company's "whats," you had better be aware of how they might alter its compliance with relevant laws.

Title III of the Sarbanes-Oxley Act of 2002, otherwise known as SOX, provides a dramatic example of the impact a new law can have on business. Enacted in the wake of the Enron and other corporate financial scandals at the dawn of the 21st century, SOX suddenly put senior executives in the unwonted position of having to take individual personal responsibility for the "accuracy and completeness" of their organizations' financial reports.

The truth is, many had no in-depth knowledge of their companies' **Disclose-Financial-Data** "what." The new law touched off a frantic scramble to correct that deficiency.

Of course, if some high-flying executives had seen the light before the government agents came calling, they might have avoided horrendous personal and corporate losses, thus erasing the need for new regulations in the first place. In today's world, though, virtually all "whats" of any consequence are subject to one or another regulation.

Compliance has been made even more complex and difficult by globalization. For example, after Congress passed the Internet gambling law, the World Trade Organization (WTO) ruled the measure illegal under the 1994 General Agreement on Trade in Services. The European Union filed a protest. Critics charged that the new law, promoted as an effort to reduce the social damage caused by gambling addiction, was actually intended to protect traditional American betting interests from competition by new online operations. As of late 2008, the conflict remained unresolved.

Intrade has managed to survive, gradually attracting new non-American members to replace those lost because of the congressional action. But the effects of the federal government's midnight lawmaking are still being felt.

Here's another company history that looks at compliance from a different vantage point.

MATCHING LAWS AND "WHATS"

From 2003 to 2006, a major American vehicle manufacturer chalked up double-digit gains in revenue and net income. In 2007, both plummeted. Why? Because when customers learned that new Environmental Protection Agency (EPA) emission standards were to take effect in 2007, many did their buying earlier than usual, sending the company's financial results on a roller-coaster ride.

In recent years, the company has been bombarded by an ever-growing list of government regulations, in Europe as well as the United States. Besides suffering the unintended sales and earnings consequences of the EPA ruling, its own cost of compliance has grown, too—at what one executive called "an unacceptable rate." He attributed the runaway expense to company uncertainty over where compliance efforts should best be focused. "As a result," our source said, "we have to 'boil the ocean' and go business unit by business unit, country unit by country unit, and department by department. That makes for a very long and costly journey."

The journey was greatly improved when the company began focusing its efforts on key "whats." To start, it identified and analyzed the business "whats" that are most vital to its success. A master list of "whats" helped company leaders determine the performance level and cost of each of these essential desired outcomes, and the appropriate regulations were electronically attached to each. When regulations and "whats" were matched up, it was possible to recognize the weak spots that might lead to a compliance problem and to plan new compliance initiatives accordingly.

I should note that if the regulation is particularly complicated and affects a number of "whats"—like SOX, for example—the mapping approach makes it much easier to measure the potential cost and effectiveness of a wide-scale initiative. It is worth noting that many of the biggest enterprise resource planning (ERP) software products in use at some of the world's biggest organizations so heavily intermingle an organization's "whats" as to make it a gigantic and expensive annual undertaking just to understand compliance status.

HOW TO RETHINK YOUR "WHATS"

To cope with government rules and laws, I suggest that you start by dividing your "whats" into three categories: those that have compliance issues, those that don't, and those that you're uncertain about and require further study. Simply recognizing which category a "what" belongs in is an important step, because it can reinforce or upset tentative decisions you've reached based on the lenses of value, performance, interconnectedness, and predictability.

You're not, I trust, going to proceed with a change after discovering that the target "whats" have existing or potential compliance problems. The existing issues have to be eliminated, and the potential issues clarified.

When there remains some uncertainty as to compliance, the predictability lens of the "whats" should come into play. If a "what" is also unpredictable, the risk of an unpleasant surprise that might move it out of compliance might be too high to proceed.

Note: In analyzing the legal status of your "whats," do not limit the examination to high-value ones alone. Being noncompliant in a low-value "what" can inflict major damage on your business.

With the addition of compliance to your store of lenses, you have all the tools needed to rethink your business. Now you're ready for a dry run. Each of the next two chapters details a single company story, its organization and behavior analyzed in terms of its "whats." Examining the details of two successfully rethought businesses can help you cope with the challenges of an uncertain economy and an ever more competitive future. First up is ING DIRECT.

EIGHT

Revolutionary Rethinking at ING DIRECT

"We cannot direct the wind,
but we can adjust the sails."

–Bertha Calloway

IN THE TIME OF THE Roman Empire, money chang-
ers set up shop in courtyards where they conducted
their business on a long bench called a bancu. In
Renaissance Florence, business loans were made
across a banco, a desk covered by a green cloth. So it
was inevitable that the builders of the echoing 19th-
century marble temples to Mammon, intent on
awing the public as well as their commercial clients,
would call their edifices "banks." And if any single
word described the banking process in those days,
it was "static." Bankers were set in their ways.

The 20th century ushered in change that shook up
the bankers' world. Technology in the form of wire
transfers, telephone banking, and the ATM transformed many of the "hows" in the industry. Banks
began to shed their awesome trappings, woo their
customers, and imitate retail stores.

Then, in the new millennium, still another shock
wave rippled across traditional banking operations
in the United States: It was called ING DIRECT
USA, an online bank that had rethought its business, deciding to put aside the "hows" and, instead,
focus obsessively on the rapid shift in the "whats"
that had become most valuable to customers. This
revolutionary bank has become a role model for creative cost-cutting and significant innovation.

Based in Wilmington, Delaware, ING DIRECT
USA is a division of the Dutch conglomerate ING

Groep NV, an insurance and banking colossus. ING DIRECT, launched in September 2000 by its chairman, president, and CEO Arkadi Kuhlmann, was envisioned as the fast-food version of banking: high volume, low margin. There would be no branches—all business would be conducted by phone or Internet—and the only product at first was a savings account with an annual interest rate of 6.5 percent, far higher than a customer could finagle at a more traditional "branched" institution.

Beyond that, there were no fees, no required minimum balances, no ATMs, no perks for big depositors, and definitely no handholding for difficult customers. Those who complained too much or stayed on the phone too long were invited to take their business elsewhere (very different from how Dell handles and values its **Resolve-Customer-Questions/Complaints** "what," as discussed earlier). As Kuhlmann explained it: "The business is not based on relationships; it's based on a commodity product. We need to keep expenses down, which doesn't work when customers want a lot of empathic contact." That policy initially saved the bank an estimated $1 million a year.

At the time, branch banks were falling all over themselves to offer customers a dizzying array of products and frills, ranging from gaudily personalized checks to extended lobby hours. But Kuhlmann took the opposite tack. He rethought the banking business, choosing a stripped-down, one-size-fits-all business model that focused on the right "whats"—and he scored. Today, ING DIRECT is the biggest U.S. online bank by far, with $80 billion in assets, and it is adding 100,000 customers a month.

Before we burrow too deep into the details of ING DIRECT's success, though, let's dial back to examine a critical change in the industry in recent years—the advent of online banking.

Historically, retail banking was largely about location. Sure, banking was a commodity service, but people still formed relationships with their local branches, and proximity was largely the reason for choosing which company to bank with. Then, when the ATM introduced a very different "how" for **Deposit-Funds**, **Withdraw-Funds**, and other "whats," it decimated the customer/teller relationship, and it wasn't long before online bill paying and automatic check depositing made it possible to go for weeks or more without ever visiting a bank at all. Result: The personal relationship many customers had with their banks was severed.

Ironically, as online services were dissolving relationships, they were also making banks stickier, because customers found it increasingly cumbersome to switch when there were so many automated deposit, payment, and withdrawal services. Still, retail banks had to wonder how they were going to win new customers now that location no longer mattered. Free checking and similar perks were nonstarters, amounting to little more than what the ancient Romans called *panem et circenses* (bread and circuses)—low-cost, low-quality diversions meant to distract people from more important matters. The commodity service that retail banking had become didn't distinguish one customer from the next. Making their money mostly on volume, the banks didn't care who did business with them as long as they could profit from the customer's assets under management.

ING DIRECT rethought this lackluster model and its accompanying "whats" and "hows." To help customers save while making more money itself, ING DIRECT lowered its operating costs by limiting its product offerings and focusing on giving customers great returns. In more graphic, detailed terms, here is how the ING DIRECT model differs from other retail banks:

Arkadi Kuhlmann learned financial discipline as a newspaper delivery boy in Toronto, Canada, the country of his birth. He earned bachelor's and master's degrees in business at the University of Western Ontario and taught college economics before switching to banking, a career move he attributes to the need to finance his social life. He rose through the ranks rapidly, landing executive posts with several institutions. At 33, Kuhlmann was a vice president of the Royal Bank of Canada and had his own corporate dining room.

In 1996, this grown-up whiz kid joined ING to create, in Canada, the first ING DIRECT. The parent company hoped to expand globally without a huge investment in a branch network, using a unique, stripped-down business model—and the required collection of "whats" and "hows"—along the lines of IKEA or Southwest Airlines. In ING DIRECT'S case, that meant no "whats" involving paper checks (ordering, printing, processing, and so on) and no "whats" related to branches (locations, construction, employees, and such). Nor did it invest in extensive customer support, preferring to focus on giving customers the highest savings rates, the best online experience, and protection from annoying overdraft fees. In short, the only "whats" that mattered were those that helped the company make money and its customers save it. The experiment succeeded, prompting ING to try replicating it in 10 other countries, starting with the United States and with Kuhlmann at the helm.

During its first two years, the U.S. start-up lost $56 million. But Kuhlmann persevered, managing **Generate-Demand** (another "what") by heavily promoting the ING DIRECT brand with its ubiquitous logo of bright orange, the national color of the Dutch royal family. (Even Kuhlmann's Harley-Davidson motorcycle is painted in the company's trademark orange and blue.)

Convinced that he was right on target with his key performance measure of customer satisfaction related to the **Deliver-Product/Service** "what," Kuhlmann insisted that millions of Americans were just waiting for ING DIRECT's simple, efficient, egalitarian approach to banking. Sure enough, in due course, the customers—Kuhlmann's kind of customers—came running. They were early adopters, comfortable with cell phones and e-mail, yet also financially conservative and wary of impulse buying.

To entice and then satisfy these people, ING DIRECT constantly monitored the performance of its **Deliver-Product/Service** "whats," a key one being **Manage-Transaction**. One of the ways that ING DIRECT increased customer satisfaction and lowered the costs of the **Manage-Transaction** "what" was to change a "how," namely having the customer do the work instead of a bank employee. Today, 75 percent of all transactions are done online with no, or only limited, support from ING staffers.

A noteworthy lesson emerges here: ING's **Manage-Transaction** "what" joins the ATM and the various "whats" involved with airport check-in as a very compelling example of processing work that people have rethought to their great advantage. Although the actual outcome hasn't changed (people still get cash from their banks or boarding passes for a flight or outsize interest rates from ING), the nature of these transactions has changed radically.

Although much of what Kuhlmann did at ING DIRECT was aimed at slashing costs, he actually increased his targeted investments in innovation to nurture the specific type of relationship he sought to have with customers. For instance, to guarantee online customers the fastest and smoothest experience possible, the company paid special attention to one of the "children"—called **Plan-and-Manage-the-Business**—that was listed under the primary "what." ING also made sure that **Manage-Information-Technology-Services** didn't become a problem child by buying and leasing state-of-the-art technology, regularly updating it, and keeping its people well versed on its use.

Just as the bank made sure its technical resources stayed up-to-date, it concentrated on another "what," **Manage-Human-Resources**, by rigorously screening and training new hires, particularly those dealing directly with telephone customers. Specifically ruling out bankers per se, Kuhlmann recruited dancers and jazz musicians, among others—people he thought would be free of what he considered banking's bad habits. They had to be polite but businesslike, good listeners but firm about moving a business encounter along briskly. To this day, the CEO personally meets with all new hires to make sure they measure up to ING DIRECT's standard: "driven, passionate, and a creative thinker." To break the ice at these meetings, the boss has been known to read palms, a skill he picked up from his European grandmother.

Kuhlmann built his thrift gospel into ING DIRECT's **Manage-Capital-Assets** "what." The company's headquarters is a refurbished warehouse located—where else?—on South Orange Street in the waterfront district of Wilmington. A marble-columned bank it certainly isn't, and Kuhlmann's simple office was designed to be equally un-bankerish. "We can't be avant-garde and glitzy," he said. "So we might as well be retro and unique." Since opening its doors, the company has renovated three more buildings, transforming the area into a commercial center that attracts national organizations and assures the city's continuing gratitude. It was vintage Kuhlmann: a civic gesture that won maximum benefit for his company.

The company's constant monitoring of the performance of its "whats"—in particular, **Fulfill-Demand**—gradually led Kuhlmann to modify the business model. Customers hadn't lost their taste for a direct, business-like relationship with their online bank, but they wanted more products. So Kuhlmann added first one (mortgages), then another (checking accounts)—in each case finding ways to make the most of ING DIRECT's existing "whats" while developing new ones only as needed.

Two mortgage products with differing maturities were offered in the first addition, a relatively easy one for ING DIRECT, given that most of the "whats" under **Create-New-Product/Service** already existed within the parent organization. The lesson here is that Kuhlmann added a full array of **Mortgage-Lending** "whats" to his business without having to add them to his company. In essence, ING DIRECT could offer the same commodity service that all other banks offer without shifting the company's focus away from what it really cared about. The company could have gotten these "whats" from many different places; it was simply most convenient and cost-effective to leverage its corporate connection and borrow from its parent. As I pointed out in Chapter 4, "Second—Know What You Are (and Aren't) Good At," company leaders need to be keenly aware of the connections among their "whats"—most definitely including their links with a parent organization. If efficiency is to be served, there can be no reluctance about leveraging a parental connection.

The ability to add and remove "whats" easily gives companies a degree of agility that was all but non-existent just a decade ago. Part of the reason, of course, has been the surge of technological progress. Microsoft's S+S approach, for example, has made it much simpler to comprehend and manipulate the network of "whats" that underpin a company.

ING DIRECT offered only a five-year and a seven-year mortgage. The company's reasoning: Most people refinance within seven years, so why should they pay higher interest for a traditional 30-year mortgage? And in keeping with the company's mission, ING DIRECT mortgages have no application fees and surprisingly low interest rates, down payments, and closing costs. The low rates and fees are possible, in part, because of the company's **Process-Mortgage-Application** "what"; its Minnesota center is all electronic without a paper file in sight.

Early on, Kuhlmann swore he would never offer checking accounts. "I don't know how to create a good value proposition and make money with checking," he told a reporter. "It's the number one area where you destroy good will from customers." Inevitably, he explained, banks would end up levying late charges and fees, which the customers "always see as a bait-and-switch."

But in 2007, after revisiting the "what" of **Create-New-Product/Service**, and its related customer-satisfaction metric, ING DIRECT gave its customers a way to pay their bills by introducing Electric Orange, the nation's first all-electronic checking account. The company met customer demand while still sticking to its basic online "what," defined as quality and cost benefits for the customer. Now ING DIRECT clients can pay by check—but only the electronic variety that sends funds directly to another person's bank account. Fund validation takes place in real time, thus preventing the overdrafts and their requisite fees that Kuhlmann so despises.

The contrast between the electronic check and its paper counterpart is interesting and instructive. Both serve the same **Withdraw-Funds** "what," but customers must keep track of their own bank balance when they write offline checks. Rather than give customers control of the **Manage-Transaction** "what" discussed earlier, ING DIRECT has changed who controls the **Validate-Available-Funds** piece of its parent's **Withdraw-Funds** "what." Otherwise, the **Withdraw-Funds** "what" has been left intact, meaning no processes are needed to deal with bounced checks, which ordinarily requires an entire department.

Other Orange products—including CDs, retirement accounts, and investment accounts—have followed ING DIRECT's mortgage and checking services. Ingdirect.com urges customers to "invest in an 'all-in-one' fund or build your own 'a la carte' portfolio." The additional online options widen customer choice through products that, in many cases, were already part of the parent company's banking structure. Once again, the company wisely opted to obtain these "whats" in the most simple, convenient, and cost-effective way: It borrowed from its parent. Mutual funds, for example, are provided by ING DIRECT Securities, a subsidiary of the bank and a registered broker-dealer. The funds are not FDIC-insured, however.

ING DIRECT has also mustered its "whats" to create its own Orange-flavored version of a physical bank branch that it calls a "café." While the "whats" of a retail bank are mostly transactional, with some elements of a relationship, Kuhlmann recognized that the performance of ING's **Sell-Product/ Service** "what," which depended on having friendly and efficient employees, was actually more differentiating than the product itself. In the ING café, one can have a sandwich and coffee, watch television, access the Internet, buy products ranging from reading glasses to mountain bikes, and chat with a sales representative about ING DIRECT products or attend occasional seminars led by Michael Rubin, author of *Beyond Paycheck to Paycheck!* As of the summer of 2007, the company had cafés in Chicago, Los Angeles, New York, Philadelphia, and Wilmington.

Despite all the changes, Arkadi Kuhlmann still insists that ING DIRECT's basic strategy remains the same: "Our mission is to lead Americans back to savings." His bank promotes financial literacy, he points out, and his high savings interest rates and the simplicity of his products are intended to "convince you that it's cool to save."

The wisdom of Kuhlmann's approach was apparent at the beginning of October 2007, when the worldwide credit drought brought down NetBank, the nation's oldest online bank. NetBank held roughly $700 million in mortgages, many of them subprime. When the housing market slumped, NetBank's mortgagees defaulted at a rate that forced federal regulators to administer last rites and close it down.

And in a ritual that alarmed media savants but rescued depositors, the regulators doled out NetBank's remains to its healthiest rivals, notably ING DIRECT, now the online banking industry's top player. ING DIRECT took on $1.4 billion of NetBank deposits and 104,000 of its depositors, for which it paid $14 million, or 1 percent of the total deposit value. In addition, ING DIRECT acquired $724 million of NetBank's assets, for which it paid nothing. None of the acquired assets were mortgages. Adhering to its strategy, ING DIRECT wanted no part of NetBank's mortgage loans, which the regulators finally persuaded another bank to buy. "We will not buy bad portfolios," Kuhlmann said flatly. "We have no subprime business at all."

Small wonder that Wall Street promptly issued a vote of confidence in Kuhlmann's parent company, ING Groep. The Dutch company's U.S. shares rose briskly to nearly $46 from $44 and change the day NetBank was closed. Just a year later, however, the world's metastasizing financial crisis enfolded ING Groep, too. Even though it was adequately capitalized, rising alarm over financial institutions in general threatened to swamp ING. The Dutch government stepped in with a 10 billion-euro infusion, however, while leaving top management in place, moves that were taken as positives by the market.

ING DIRECT DID WHAT?

To recap what Kuhlmann has accomplished by rethinking ING DIRECT, let's start by noting that he saw the Internet as making location totally irrelevant to retail banking. Given that prior to the emergence of the ATM, location had been the one thing that differentiated players in the commodity banking business, Kuhlmann's prescience was huge. Seeing opportunity, he looked at how retail banking was done and ditched formerly important "hows" in favor of focusing on more important "whats." He slashed costs by forgoing brick-and-mortar branches, lowering customer-support performance measures, and revolutionizing operations through the introduction of easy online customer transactions. In addition, Kuhlmann's online model prevented bounced checks, allowing him to eliminate the need for a department to handle such checks—yet another money saver.

Finally, Kuhlmann's investments in information technology and ING DIRECT's ability to pay a higher interest rate to customers enabled it to establish a clear brand identity in the marketplace. That identity, in turn, made it clear what ING DIRECT values.

In a different part of the business landscape, Vern Raburn was piloting his start-up along a path somewhat similar to ING DIRECT's. His product, a small general-aviation jet, was designed to be inexpensive in a world of luxe, standardized where its rivals were custom-built. In the chapter just ahead, I'll describe how Raburn managed his "whats" and separated them from his "hows" to attain his goal—until he stumbled over the hard work of execution.

NINE

Rethinking at Eclipse

*"I have found adventure in flying,
in world travel, in business, and
even close at hand. Adventure is
a state of mind and spirit."*

–Jacqueline Cochran

BACK IN THE 1970S, people laughed when PC pioneers predicted that a computer would soon adorn every desk in America. Vern Raburn had the last laugh. As Microsoft's vice president in charge of application software, Raburn helped make that prophecy come true.

Three decades later, Raburn found another career, general aviation, and this time he combined predicting with rethinking. Anticipating that private aviation was ripe for revolution, he theorized that his own new six-seat, twin-engine Very Light Jet (VLJ) could be perfectly positioned to take advantage of the new trend. That's because his aircraft would cost half as much to buy and operate as any of its private-jet rivals. To tip the scales in his direction, Raburn assembled an impressive collection of manufacturing "whats" while discarding some not-so-golden oldies, and he reimagined many of the "hows." As it turned out, Raburn stumbled when it came to the hard business of execution, but his clear vision and his decision to rethink provides a worthwhile lesson for businesses everywhere.

Raburn's first epiphany was borrowed from Silicon Valley. "Historically in aviation," he explains, "the term 'value proposition' meant that a better plane justified a higher price. In the business I come from, it's the other way around. You make the product better, and you charge less." Raburn helped do that for computers, and it's what his Eclipse Aviation Corporation set out to do for aircraft.

Although Eclipse 500s have yet to make a big dent in today's congested skies, more than 200 have taken off across the country. Orders for 2,000 more have flooded into Eclipse headquarters in Albuquerque, New Mexico—which, by the way, is where Microsoft got its start.

Raburn initially promised an air taxi for busy executives that would cost just $900,000—less than one-third the $2.8 million price of an entry-level Cessna Citation Mustang. That high hurdle turned out to be insurmountable, and the Eclipse board replaced him as CEO after production fell behind schedule and the sticker price jumped, first to $1.5 million and then to $2.15 million. For a while, however, the start-up had the rest of the industry worried—and the threat hasn't totally dissipated. Rival makers know they can't ignore Eclipse's innovations. They must begin adapting, or else.

From the first, Raburn's timing was impeccable. Demand for the speed and convenience of personal aircraft was, and remains, intense. Businesspeople have never been so eager to avoid commercial travel. They loathe the hub-and-spoke system that requires extra connections, and they're fed up with shrinking seats and leg room, canceled flights, missed meetings, rude flight attendants, hostile passengers, security delays, and short hops that become two-day marathons. To bypass these ulcer-enhancing and money-losing fixtures of modern travel, companies are buying their own planes or joining time-share plans that cut charter costs.

Aside from business ambition, Raburn had a personal reason for developing the 500. An avid pilot, he wanted a smaller, affordable jet for himself. Flying is in his genes. His father was once Douglas Aircraft's chief engineer, and his uncle was a Cessna engineer during World War II. Raburn was seven years old the first time he flew—aboard a Central Airlines DC-3, sitting on the pilot's lap. As a teenager, he mowed lawns and delivered newspapers to pay for flying lessons. Weak eyesight barred him from professional piloting, but he studied aeronautical engineering in college and switched to industrial technology only when hard times hit the aviation industry.

While rising in the Microsoft ranks, Raburn spent his off-hours in the air. "By the time I started working for the Paul Allen Group," he recalls, "I had more than 5,000 hours of flying time. I had flown everything from airliners to corporate jets, from World War II bombers to fighters and everything else in between."

Raburn loved the adventurous side of flying, but not the business side; it was hugely expensive and way too complicated. Merely buying his Cessna Citation jet was a study in overconsumption. "It took me and my wife all day to specify the airplane because we had to pick out coverings for 23 different surfaces in the interior," he says. "We two customers were surrounded by a dozen people urging us to choose this fabric or that leather. The decisions were more complex than building a house."

More and more, Raburn perceived aviation as a paradox of high tech and low vision, an industry so myopic that it teemed with unnoticed business opportunities that cried out for rethinking. Raburn did more than take notice; he also had the drive to act on those opportunities. He was a born analyst of aviation "whats" and the attendant "hows" needed to produce the best results.

Two marketing realities, in particular, struck him: First, airline indifference absolutely enrages certain travelers, notably those whose livelihoods depend on selling their time profitably. Among those who must travel quickly and economically, Raburn lists "accountants and lawyers, car dealers, and executives of construction companies. For them, an alternate form of mass transportation has massive appeal," he says.

Second, such people generally have only one alternative to commercial flights—private corporate jets—and most of them lack anything close to the personal wealth required to buy one. Right now, the cheapest Learjet costs about $6 million, while Gulfstreams start at $25 million. Gulfstream has an internal tool it uses to predict buyers, Raburn says:

"They call it 'Egometrics,' and use it to determine when, or if, they will close the sale on a $50 million airplane. That gives you some idea of the wackiness of a marketplace that sells $50 million vehicles to transport one owner's body."

In 1997, Raburn's imagination took flight with dreams of the Eclipse. Aimed at all those unhappy business travelers (an ever-growing market), Raburn envisioned his invention flying all across America as a readily accessible air taxi for middle-income travelers or an economy jet for affluent private owners whose pockets still weren't deep enough to cover a multimillion-dollar Cessna Citation or Learjet. But creating the Eclipse would be a daunting challenge. No part of the existing aerospace industry had either the ability or the desire to produce any such aircraft.

Analyzing what he was up against, Raburn discovered that the "what" called **Manufacture-Product** in the aircraft industry is unlike that of any other business—be it automobiles, computers, or consumer electronics. He calls the business "a low-volume industry that survives principally on craftsmanship and massive levels of tribal knowledge." It was also dauntingly customized: "In some ways, I found a bespoke industry that made everything almost by hand, despite all its huge machines."

The aerospace industry seemed ripe for invasion by new players with new technology and Darwinian

views of competition. But Raburn noted two cost-
ballooning obstacles for new contenders: "First,
this is an industry with radical, significant regulatory oversight." Only the pharmaceutical industry
is subjected to a comparable degree of government scrutiny. The commendable purpose is public
safety, but the cost of compliance is high. According
to Raburn, "We spent $100 million on getting our
airplane certified by the FAA, and that was just the
beginning of endless compliance costs for training,
operations, and so on."

The second obstacle for aspiring entrants is the
peculiar state of the general aviation market. Production of private aircraft peaked in 1978, when 25
manufacturers turned out a mere 18,000 airplanes.
By 1992, the industry had dwindled to half as many
manufacturers producing only 600 airplanes. Then,
at the turn of the century, came an unexpected
rebirth as stock-market bubbles spawned more
super-rich Americans with a hunger for super-toys.
General aviation became a luxury marketplace
conspicuously uninterested in the growing needs
of mere mortals.

As Raburn saw it, starting from scratch with Eclipse
would give him an actual advantage: It would free
him from all the bad habits, costly processes, and
heavy overhead structures that prevented the luxury aerospace industry from serving his target customers. In rethinking the private aviation business

to include more people, Raburn's challenge would be to identify the exact "whats" necessary for success while jettisoning the rest.

Take toilets, for instance. **Install-Toilet** seemed to be a given "what," and bathrooms are pretty much standard in multiple-passenger planes. But from Raburn's vantage, toilets had two major drawbacks—extra weight and cost. Keeping both numbers as low as possible would directly increase the chances of success for the Eclipse. More importantly, he reasoned, passengers could do without a bathroom break on the typical short hops of, say, 40 to 80 minutes that his super-fast VLJ was designed to fly.

Better yet, Raburn's decision to flush the **Install-Toilet** "what" had a ripple effect that streamlined the entire design and manufacturing process. Now he could also eliminate interconnected "whats" such as the following:

- **Design-Toilet**
- **Procure-Toilet-Parts**
- **Assemble-Raw-Materials**
- **Customize-Product**

Obviously, the removal of each of these "whats" ramped up efficiency and chopped costs.

Often working by trial and error, Raburn borrowed production ideas from companies in other fields—including high-tech, high-volume stars like Carrier, Intel, and Toyota. He also improvised his own techniques. Gradually, he streamlined the "whats" required to manufacture his unique aircraft.

Armed with a business plan and promising "a completely new kind of commercial air travel, a limousine of the air," Raburn solicited investors who owned personal aircraft and thus had firsthand knowledge of their shortcomings. In May 1998, he launched his company with a public stock offering that raised an initial $60 million. In August 2002, the Eclipse 500 made its first flight, the start of a scheduled 16-month testing program leading toward FAA certification. Three months later, Raburn called time out. A series of failures with the EJ22 turbofan engine—from fires to broken fan blades—forced him to abandon it.

A large infusion of cash was needed to save the company. Some board members wavered, and key employees had to be persuaded to stay. But Al Mann, a billionaire entrepreneur, handed over $50 million of his own money and helped corral another $37 million from others. Mann ended up owning 30 percent of the company. Raburn offered to return all customer deposits, but only 60 out of 2,100 signed-up customers took him up on it. So, in spite of imperfections in the execution at Eclipse,

Raburn won validation for the way in which he
rethought private aircraft production, blending
cost-cutting measures with significant innovation.

In September 2006, the 500 received FAA certification, powered by a Pratt & Whitney Canada
replacement engine.

In the executive aircraft industry, where verti-
cal integration has been the accepted production
model, Raburn broke with tradition by rethinking his "whats" and outsourcing subcategories of
Manufacture-Product such as **Fabricate-Tail-
Assembly**, which he knew could be done cheaper
and better elsewhere, freeing up his people to focus
on the "whats" they could do best. A veritable United
Nations of vendors located in countries ranging
from Canada to Japan to Britain to Chile turn out
the engine, wings, nose cone, and other essential
components.

Eclipse itself owns the "whats" of **Manufacture-
Product** and **Test-Product**, but it doesn't stand by
passively waiting for parts to arrive. To maintain
quality throughout, all suppliers are required to
police every "what" using statistical controls that
spot manufacturing glitches. Obviously, Eclipse
pursued a course that Boeing, to its chagrin, passed
up in producing its ill-starred 787 Dreamliner; suppliers should be locked into performance agreements that protect every mission-critical "what."

At Eclipse, engineers constantly monitor the numbers to make sure suppliers are living up to their agreements.

The controls on suppliers reflect performance definitions and metrics the company has developed for all of its "whats," whether they are carried out at Eclipse or are outsourced to a supplier. Performance metrics, for example, revealed that when a mechanic had to retrieve parts or tools located more than eight feet from his post, the performance of the **Manufacture-Product** "what" suffered. To prevent it, Eclipse carefully laid out its mechanic workstations with all tools and tasks placed within an eight-foot radius of the person on the job.

The traditional assembly line is the "how" that most aircraft companies use for the **Manufacture-Product** "what." But Eclipse achieves greater flexibility by bringing its people to the evolving aircraft, arranging the planes in a U-shaped manufacturing cell with tooling platforms that move on dollies. In another departure from the norm, the Eclipse **Connect-Skin-to-Skeleton** "what" dispenses with the traditional riveted "how" in favor of laying out the aluminum skin in a mold and then building the skeleton into it. That innovation gives the manufacturer better control over the plane's final shape and produces a cabin that can withstand higher levels of pressurization—not to mention that it saves time, weight, and production costs. On most

aircraft production lines, formed parts far out-
number high-precision machined components,
but Eclipse has reversed the ratio to make sure
assemblies fit together properly the first time. And
whereas most of its rivals make major use of composite materials, Eclipse has opted for components
machined from single bars of aluminum that are
lighter, stronger, and more cost-effective.

Because Eclipse aims for high-volume, low-cost
production, standardization is the rule. At competitors' plants, each plane moving along the assembly
line has its own set of drawings conforming to a
customer's choices from among a wide variety of
options. The sticker price doesn't begin to reflect
the total cost of adding a host of pricey options, and
customers pay dearly for all this customization.
That's not a problem at Eclipse because most of the
available options are already built into the basic aircraft. It's an efficient and economical way of working that allows a single crew to assemble a frame in
one shift while a complete interior can be installed
in 45 minutes.

In pursuing its central "whats"—**Create-New-
Product** and **Manufacture-Product**—Eclipse has
further leapfrogged standard aviation practices via
a host of new "hows." Few are as impressive, however, as its use of friction stir welding to build fuse-
lages. The technique employs a rapidly rotating tool
to cut completely through one piece of aluminum

and partially through another while the heat and deformation cause the two pieces to meld into one along a continuous seam. Using this "how" in its **Connect-Skin-to-Skeleton** "what" allows Eclipse to eliminate thousands of rivets, drastically reducing costs and weight and delivering stronger and smoother joints at a rate 10 times faster than manual riveting. Friction stir welding is also far more accurate because the cutting tools are controlled by computers rather than human hands.

One of Eclipse's abiding principles, Raburn says, is a belief that "innovation and disruptive technology can create a new value proposition, which will, in turn, expand existing markets and create whole new markets." The electronic systems his engineers and suppliers have fashioned for the 500 are a case in point.

Missing from Eclipse instrument panels are the round dials that commercial pilots once constantly eyed for critical information. A generation ago, the airlines replaced the dials with computer-mediated *multifunction displays* (MFD). But until the Eclipse arrived, general aviation had lagged behind. Raburn's **Assemble-Instrument-Panel** "what" dispenses with nearly all traditional avionics items, along with their complex mechanisms and costly maintenance requirements, in favor of circuit boards and MFDs that deliver far more information in a better organized, more accessible form.

So different is cockpit fabrication for the 500 that Eclipse had to add a **Train-New-Pilot** "what" as a subcategory under **Fulfill-Demand**. The elaborate training program for buyers, including veteran pilots, is handled by the company itself. Indeed, Raburn has created the most comprehensive flight-training operation in general aviation. The two-week course, as described by the company, includes "self-paced, computer-based study; high-altitude physiology training; and unexpected-situations hands-on training," as well as mentoring and annual brush-up sessions. Eclipse has two full-motion flight simulators and two more are on the way. The whole program was housed in a new 41,500-square-foot training facility in September 2007.

Yet another of Eclipse's key in-house "whats" is the design of the plane's engine fire-control system—the first such new design to win FAA approval since 1954. The **Assemble-Fire-Extinguisher** "what" relies on a new, more cost-effective "how" called PhostrEx, an extinguishing chemical that is superior to the Halon commonly used in other systems. The more powerful PhostrEx—two teaspoons is the equivalent of 2.5 cups of Halon—requires a much lighter and smaller delivery system, helping to shrink the weight of the 500's entire fire-control system to just seven-tenths of a pound. In addition, the far simpler system can be contained in a no-touch canister for ten years, whereas Halon systems require periodic and costly maintenance.

Eclipse's grasp of, and focus on, its "whats" leads naturally to straight talk and transparency—uncommon qualities in an industry given to hype. For example, general-aviation companies have routinely announced the imminence of first flights or FAA certification. When the dates come and go without the promised event, the spinners' silence speaks louder than their blather ever could.

Eclipse, by contrast, posts an interactive version of its master schedule on its Web site, Eclipseaviation.com. When it misses a target date, the delay is announced along with the reason for it. In the spring of 2007, for example, the company experienced serious production difficulties. Raburn posted a lengthy and detailed explanation on the site, listing each problem followed by his plan to correct it. In general, he blamed supplier shortcomings but also owned up to design glitches and "leadership oversights."

Transparency, Raburn believes, is not just a matter of rectitude; it is also indispensable to the trust that bonds his company with its suppliers, customers, and investors. "We felt this was another thing that desperately needs to be changed in this industry," he explains. Trust is essential to maintaining healthy, productive connections among the "whats" inside a company and those outside at its suppliers.

Sadly, however, there have been far too many occasions for transparent postings on Eclipseaviation.com. First came the engine problems and certification delays, then the glitches in the supply chain, followed by production snafus. Raburn initially promised to churn out 1,000 planes per year, but after two years, only 235 had been delivered (259 by the end of 2008)—and the costs kept ballooning.

Then, in July 2008, a group of investors known as ETIRC Aviation (ETIRC stands for European Technology and Investment Research Center) staged a coup while Raburn was attending an air show with his friend and flying buddy, actor John Travolta. The board voted to demote Raburn to vice chairman and adviser. Roel Pieper, chairman of ETIRC, which owns a $100 million equity stake in Eclipse, took over as the company's acting chief executive.

Pieper has vowed to make Raburn's vision a reality, but he's clearly flying in a turbulent environment. Not surprisingly given Raburn's real achievements, Eclipse has plenty of competitors eager to join the race by rethinking their own aircraft as very light jets. They include old-timers like Cessna and Brazil's Embraer as well as giant newcomer Honda Motors, which has a prototype plane that is even faster (though pricier) than the 500. Not least is Adam Aircraft, a major rival upstart based in Evergreen, Colorado, and bankrolled by the Hunt family of Texas oil fame. Adam has 75 orders from Pogo Jet, an air-taxi operator scheduled to launch in 2009. Pogo is the progeny of two well-known airline veterans, Robert Crandall and Donald Burr, the former CEOs of American Airlines and People Express, respectively.

None of the troubles and threats besetting Eclipse can dim Vern Raburn's accomplishments. By rethinking his company's required "whats" and adopting state-of-the-art "hows," he has opened a new world of opportunity for Eclipse, for general aviation, and for the flying public. Most profoundly, of course, he has validated a business model that targets a long-ignored market and brings a laser focus to the task of capturing and serving that market. Pieper himself credits Raburn with inventing the whole VLJ category and "achieving what the industry did not think possible." Whatever happens to the Eclipse 500, no one can take that away from Vern Raburn.

ECLIPSE AVIATION DID WHAT?

Much like we saw with ING DIRECT, Eclipse Aviation rethought a number of aviation "whats" and "hows," managing, in the process, to cut costs in a number of key areas, including the customization of aircraft options and the total elimination of all "whats" related to having a lavatory on the plane. Consequently, production time was radically reduced as well. The rethinking also enabled Eclipse to invest in innovation—for instance, in the way it connected the aircraft skin to the skeleton, thus making the plane lighter and eliminating production steps. All this was accomplished on the now-proven assertion that some people are willing to give up certain luxuries and conveniences to access personal air travel at a still high, but decidedly more affordable price than what had previously been available.

The story of Eclipse Aviation and Vern Raburn offers a great lesson in asking questions about what the customer values and rethinking to accommodate those desires at a lower cost.

While Vern Raburn was dreaming of making the skies much friendlier for middle- and upper-income airline customers, two Seattle-based entrepreneurs were inventing their own highflier, a stupendously popular board game called Cranium. The next chapter relates how Richard Tait and Whit Alexander parlayed their focus on "whats" and "hows" into one of the fastest-selling new products in the history of independent game creators.

TEN

Rethinking at Cranium

*"If life doesn't offer a game worth
playing, then invent a new one."*

–Anthony J. D'Angelo

BACK IN 1997, Richard Tait was a dynamic Scottish immigrant working for Microsoft in Seattle and amusing friends with his unwavering ability to lose at Scrabble. After a particularly humiliating defeat, Tait asked himself, "Why isn't there a game that gives everyone a chance to shine?" He convinced Whit Alexander, an old friend, to help him develop a board game that would challenge multiple talents and let all the players win. They called it Cranium.

A decade later, the inventive partners were comfortably seated atop an organization that had sold more than 22 million games, books, and toys in 40 countries and 10 languages. Their Seattle-based enterprise is now one of the most successful ventures in the history of independent game companies, and the Cranium game holds the sales speed record among independents.

How did Tait and Alexander wend their way through a crowded marketplace to reach their current eminence? By tapping the brain matter encased in their own craniums to rethink their business, and then eliminating, adding to, and reinventing their "whats" and "hows" to create a business model that is unique among their peers.

Cranium is exactly the game Richard Tait had in mind when he despaired of ever winning at Scrabble. It has something for just about everyone, from word puzzles and fact-based questions to sculpting, sketching, acting, and even humming. And for a growing band of Craniacs (not to be confused with the sinister Craniac robots that inhabit Nickelodeon's animated ChalkZone series), the game is addictive.

To grasp the extent of their rethinking, it's crucial to understand how the minds of Tait and Alexander work. First, they know exactly what they value and never deviate from their designated path. Second, their singular focus on accomplishing their high value "whats" makes them flexibly pragmatic, thus allowing them to avoid getting bogged down in unimportant "hows."

Even as a boy delivering newspapers in Scotland, Richard Tait showed a knack for spotting and capturing opportunity. After noticing that many of his customers ate rolls and bacon while reading the paper, he began delivering those provisions along with the papers. Despite having an affinity for pounds and pence, young Richard nixed his parents' suggestion that he become an accountant. Too dreary, said the boy, who yearned to be a musician. Dad wasn't keen on music, but he used it as bait to steer his son toward technology: He gave Richard a kit for building a synthesizer. The ploy worked, and Richard wound up studying computer science at Dartmouth College in Hanover, New Hampshire, and going on to work at Microsoft.

Whit Alexander was chasing a degree in African studies at Georgetown University when he heard a fascinating guest lecturer say he was starting an economic consulting firm in Africa. Alexander signed on, initially for no salary, and spent years there, eventually working as an independent contractor. Along the way, he became interested in software and computer mapping. Back in the States, working on a master's degree at the University of Washington, he saw a notice that Microsoft needed a cartographer for a digital encyclopedia. Off he went.

Having become friends while working on the encyclopedia, Tait and Alexander agreed to go into business together in 1997. Given their techie credentials, the two naturally thought of designing a video game, but they had nowhere near the needed capital. Creating an adult board game would be much less expensive, they decided—a perfect example of the way the pair immediately focuses on what they want to do, not caring how they do it. If video gaming is too expensive, no problem, they reason; the "what" that matters is **Create-New-Game**, and we'll take a different route to it.

Tait had already been thinking about a left-brain, right-brain game that would call on players' different skills—logic and word play on the left, singing and drawing on the right. Then he found the work of Howard Gardner, a Harvard professor of education who defines human intelligence as a collection of multiple abilities, including musical talent, physical dexterity, linguistic skill, and spatial manipulation. Gardner, in effect, had deconstructed human intelligence and found that these abilities were the specific gears that set in motion the larger human intelligence machine. If Tait and Alexander could devise an adult board game that engaged several of these gears, left brain and right, then every player would have a chance to excel.

That was the theory—and a novel one it was for an industry built on cutthroat competition. For Tait and Alexander, the "what" labeled **Create-New-Game** took center stage, and it required the partners to combine a large dose of imagination with an intense focus on every detail of their unusual game. They knew that the industry would be looking for excuses to reject a game with no winners in the traditional sense, which meant that nothing could be left to chance.

The partners wanted their game to engage players by giving them a shot at competing in heretofore-unheard-of challenges, but there's a fine line between a unique form of fun and something that's just plain silly or weird. For example, Alexander wanted to give a player 30 seconds to sculpt a recognizable object out of clay and have the other players guess what it was. Tait didn't like that idea, convinced that adults would think playing with clay was too childish.

The partners settled their differences by adding a series of new "children" to the conventional gaming-business "whats." So the **Analyze-Gamer-Reaction** and the related **Analyze-Gamer-Interaction** subcategories gave new depth to the critically important "what" called **Create-Prototype** and **Test-Prototype**. The idea was to test every aspect of the game extensively before deciding on one approach or another. And how the Cranium team went about performing this "what" was light years from the typical focus-group experience, in which participants sit around answering questions.

At Cranium, real people didn't just talk about clay, they actually played with the stuff. And because of that hands-on approach, Tait remembers the exact moment he changed his mind and embraced Alexander's notion of having players sculpt objects out of clay: Watching a 40-year-old sink his fingers into the clay, "I looked at his eyes, and the eyes of a four-year-old looked back."

Not just any clay would do, of course. So, predictably, before the partners made their choice, they sampled dozens of scents, colors, and 10 different clay recipes. Their clay had to feel good, smell good, leave no traces on fingers, and have a long shelf life. It was clear that no feature would be overlooked in their incredibly detail-oriented rethinking of the game industry's **Create-Prototype** and **Test-Prototype** "whats."

Drawing on their Internet expertise, the pair honed their **Create-New-Game** and **Create-Prototype** "whats" by forming a kind of virtual editorial board to pass judgment on the word content of the Cranium game. Working online, seven specialists weighed in on visual arts, pop culture, and theater, among other areas. They also examined the game's questions and instructions in terms of appeal, level of difficulty, and age-appropriateness.

To determine the optimum length of time a game should run, the partners fell back on their computer knowledge and expertise. Thousands of different scenarios were created, and the dynamics of each version were explored by varying the number of questions asked, for example, or the number of people playing. To prevent one-sided results, each player was allowed to take on just a single task before the play moved on to the next person.

After all the testing, observation, and editing, the final iteration of the game required teams to advance around the board toward 'Cranium Central' by completing tasks described on Cranium cards. The game contains four decks of cards, each devoted to one aspect of intelligence: Creative Cat has players sculpting and sketching; Data Head tests their knowledge of trivia; Word Worm challenges their language skills; and Star Performer asks them to act and sing.

Creating a radically different game wasn't Tait's and Alexander's only objective. The partners also shared another dream—to make Cranium a lifestyle brand by taking it beyond board games to other kinds of activities and occasions where people meet and interact. Energized by Cranium's goal of high customer satisfaction, Tait envisioned the company's products becoming "woven into the fabric of families' lives." To that end, the partners set to work finding ways to test and improve each new product idea. And while they always came up with the design-new-game first step in the **Create-New-Game** "what," they had no qualms about outsourcing the overall Create-New-Game "what" to a trusted collaborator.

That collaborator was Andy Forrest, who, along with his partner Allen Pruzan, helped Cranium's founders build a game chest of new products following the success of the original Cranium game. Forrest remembers that, from the get-go, Richard Tait envisioned a stable of branded products—both games and other items—all linked to Gardner's multiple intelligence theory. So, unlike most game companies, his was never a business driven by a single idea. The **Create-New-Game** and **Manage-Existing-Game** "whats" gave the Cranium business legs that the vast majority of new companies lack.

"How many can you make in a year?" Tait asked at his first meeting with Forrest and Pruzan.

Cognizant that the **Market-Game** "what" was still largely focused on supplying the muscle needed to make the original Cranium game the success it was destined to be, the creative team suggested inventing perhaps two or three new games in the first year of any potential working agreement. "Two or three!" Tait shot back. "I was thinking more like fifteen." "He was pushing all the time…he's got a bigger vision in his head," Forrest says. An unabashed admirer, he describes Tait as inspiring, charismatic, and burning with uncommon passion.

Eventually, the outside creative team signed on for a five-year stint with Cranium, becoming what Forrest describes as "sort of their de facto R&D department." Having determined that outsourcing the **Create-New-Game** "what" to a high-quality partner was the best way to go, Cranium never once scrimped on quality. "They were committed to it," Forrest says, meaning that Tait and Alexander devoted both the time and the money necessary to allow their smart, capable team of collaborators to go the extra mile in developing a hit product. Forrest recalls, for example, that in designing their early games for children, Cranium Cadoo and Hullabaloo, "well over 100 play tests with kids" were conducted to get the absolutely best prototypes for each new game.

There were budgets, of course, and the Forrest-Pruzan team laid out the different cost benefits of assorted work plans. But, in Forrest's estimation, a critical piece in the success of Cranium's **Create-New-Game** "what" was the decision to give the team a cut of downstream revenues from the products they turned out. "There is a tendency for innovation to be more easily attained by people who have a stake in it," he says.

At Cranium, the "how" of game design begins, Forrest continues, with a firm knowledge of the marketplace—which, in the world of games and toys, is largely made up of moms. Mothers buy 85 percent of the products, so their likes and dislikes count for a lot. Nevertheless, a designer still has to please the eventual user of the product, so a game-design shop tries to hire an eclectic mix of people—ranging from educators and camp counselors to theater types and market analysts—to help it understand how various age groups, male and female, respond to game playing and other forms of entertainment.

An actual Cranium design session for a new game starts with "moment engineering," an exercise in imagining the pleasure each player should experience at some point in the game play. At one meeting, for instance, participants drew pictures showing a mother and her children housebound on a rainy day. The kids, all focused on a Cranium game, gave mom a high-five of approval. The goal was to spur the designers to come up with a product capable of sparking just such a moment in real game play.

When an initial game design is complete, the redesign begins—and it is crucial. The product idea, Forrest explains, "is not as important as the iteration of the idea." Each Cranium demo model thus undergoes the kind of exhaustive testing Forrest described for Hullabaloo and Cadoo. The only foolproof way to do that is by playing a game until you're sure it works—no matter how long it takes.

Play testers gather in Cranium's make-believe living room to try out a new game, with designers watching behind one-way mirrors. "Sometimes it's just painful," Richard Tait says, especially when a game inspires boredom or too much rivalry. In testing Balloon Lagoon, for instance, a game for kindergarteners, the kids had 30 seconds on an hourglass timer to try each of four activities. Almost immediately after one child would begin performing, another would start tapping the timer and shouting, "Time's almost up! Time's almost up!" The game became a tense competition. But when designers replaced the timer with a music box that played for just 30 seconds, the result was magical. Instead of heckling the players, the onlookers cheered them.

Without the **Analyze-Gamer-Reaction** "what," the designers might never have discovered the right "how"—the music box—for the Balloon Lagoon game. In which case, the game could very well have flopped. And even if it had sold, it wouldn't have fit the Cranium image.

In another example of how Cranium changes "hows" in its unorthodox approach to the make-games business, the company's model makers will often be on hand for a play-test session, so they can redesign and retest the prototype on the spot. Or maybe the prototype will be remade in 24 hours or 48 hours and put back in front of a fresh group of testers, with the process repeated over and over until the game is right. "We literally build product in between play tests," explains Forrest. "That is how we make hit products, because we know they are hits" before they leave the company shop.

Pumped up by their early and astounding success, the Cranium team has pushed its **Create-New-Game** "what" to ever greater heights. Year after year, they top themselves by improving old games, developing ever more ingenious and entertaining new ones, and successfully extending the brand to toys, books, and electronic learning. The Wonder-Works series of toys, for instance, gives youngsters a zany concept—say, an octopus riding a bicycle— that then inspires them to draw or record stories that can be shared with friends or family.

Tait and Alexander upended tradition yet again by rethinking the toy industry's **Distribute-Product** "what." Game manufacturers have traditionally relied primarily on toy stores and children's areas in department stores to lure customers to a new product. But the Cranium duo took their goods to customers wherever they might be—beginning with a coffeehouse.

With no place to sell the first 20,000 Cranium games they had confidently ordered from their manufacturer in 1998, Tait and Alexander came up with a novel "how" to accomplish the **Generate-Demand** "what," and they pitched their idea to Howard Schultz, the chairman of Starbucks. Their logic: His company had achieved success by providing a sociable environment. Cranium was a highly social game. So why not bring the game to the place where its ideal audience could be found, thereby enhancing Starbucks' ambience in the bargain? Schultz, who had an interest in one of the investment groups bankrolling Cranium, readily agreed. In no time, customers were playing the game not only in Starbucks outlets, but also in bars, homes, and airports.

The Cranium wizards also enlisted booksellers Amazon.com and Barnes & Noble—two more places they thought potential game-playing adult customers might hang out. Neither company was interested in Cranium at first. But the game's fast-rising success at Starbucks outlets across the country and the partners' perseverance carried the day. Instead of customers having to find a place to buy Cranium, the game came to the customers.

Eschewing the usual industry marketing "how" of mounting a costly advertising campaign (corporate media budgets can top $500 million a year) and wanting to reach customers in their customary locales and with a more personal message, the partners opted at first for word of mouth, free media mentions, and a radio promotion in which DJs across the country read Cranium questions and gave away Cranium games to the callers who answered correctly.

Placing Cranium in Starbucks outlets got the viral marketing campaign going, and an enthusiastic plug by actress Julia Roberts on the omnipotent Oprah television show kicked it into high gear. The company has since become a publicity legend, bolstered by free testimonials from the likes of Al Gore, who celebrated a birthday lying on the floor playing a Cranium game with his grandchildren. The media obligingly spread the story of a company that built a business on a game in which everyone wins.

After Cranium was selling briskly, its flexible founders were ready to begin re-imagining the "how" of the various "whats" involved in **Distribute-Game** and **Sell-Game**. Having sold their first million units without advertising, they switched gears and bought space. No longer intent on avoiding toy stores, they wooed and won Toys 'R' Us and Target. "We love to change the rules," Tait says.

The search for better ways to market products led Tait and Alexander to redefine the toy industry's accepted "hows" for **Generate-Demand** while embracing the "what" designated as **Manage-Partner-Relationships.** Their success in taking the Cranium game to Starbucks and Barnes & Noble customers inspired them to form relationships with other venues where families can be found, such as zoos and Hyatt Hotels & Resorts. Most Hyatt properties in the United States now greet young guests and their parents with a courtesy trial pack of Cranium games, reflecting Cranium's emphasis on reintroducing the concept of fun into family vacations. Concierges will also supply other Cranium games to families and their children, free on request.

That strategy has also worked well for Zooreka, a Cranium board game in which players swap animals, food, and shelter in their quest to create a safe zoo. To build presale buzz, the company sent complimentary copies of the game to zoos around the country, suggesting that they encourage young visitors to play Zooreka in a real zoo. In 2007, the Toy Industry Association designated Zooreka as "Toy of the Year," the fifth time a Cranium product has won the award.

Because Cranium has always been more than just a business for its founders, they have cultivated human-resource-related "whats" that combine a sense of mission with a sense of humor. As part of the company's **Recruit-New-Talent** "what," for example, every new employee receives 10 free games to give to family and friends and five more for charities. Each newcomer is also encouraged to create a unique job title, provided that it actually reflects his or her work. The results tend toward the goofy. Tait, for example, is not the CEO but, rather, the Grand Poo Bah. Whit Alexander was the Chief Noodler until he left management in 2007 to find his "next great thing." (He was still an active board member until the company was recently acquired by Hasbro.) Heather Snavely, who oversees brand communications, is "Head of the Hive." (She creates product buzz.) Every new arrival, no matter his or her position, is welcomed with the ringing of the office gong and a party.

The acronym CHIFF sums up Cranium's mission, and every employee, supplier, and partner of any kind knows exactly what it stands for: *clever, high quality, innovative, friendly,* and *fun.* Even vendors and distributors may ask if something "is CHIFF enough." Conversely, they may, on their own and without prodding or demur from Cranium, declare of some item or product detail, "No, it's not CHIFF enough." Invariably, that verdict triggers a fresh look and often a redo.

That Cranium has fulfilled its founders' dreams is a tribute to the company's steadfast commitment to CHIFF—and to its ability to keep rethinking, evolving, and reinventing key "whats." The lasting lesson is that the ability to recognize, analyze, and maximize your "whats" and "hows" is the key to corporate success in these uncertain times. It's good to remember that in business, unlike the world of Cranium, everyone is not a winner.

CRANIUM DID WHAT?

The story of Cranium has some interesting parallels to the Newman's Own story recounted in Chapter 3, "First—Identify the 'Whats' That Are Truly Valuable." Though Paul Newman and A.E. Hotchner did it for different reasons, they outsourced manufacturing and distribution because they didn't value it, whereas Richard Tait and Whit Alexander realized that their **Create-New-Game** "what" simply wasn't a core competency. Both are totally valid reasons to arrive at a similar conclusion as long as you are specific about what you value and what you can and should be good at.

From their **Create-New-Game** to **Analyze-Gamer-Reaction** to **Human-Resource** "whats," Tait and Alexander know exactly what they want to achieve and never stray from their chosen path. And whether they are talking about clay or a game's timing devices or its questions and instructions, they are adamant about the details. No feature is overlooked in their rethinking of the game industry's "whats." It is that singular focus—as exemplified by their no-fuss decision early on to forgo video gaming in favor of an adult board game—that ensures their success.

In the final chapter, I argue that successful companies have figured out how to rethink their "whats"—multiple times if need be—to cope with the ever-changing marketplace. Amazon and Procter & Gamble, both of which have escaped from "how" traps through a series of clever and astounding changes, show the way.

ELEVEN

Morph Again and Again

*"The road to success is always
under construction."*

–Arnold Palmer

WHEN SHAKESPEARE WROTE Hamlet's great solil-
oquy, "To be or not to be," he not only defined
human ambiguity, he also foreshadowed the uncertain future of the play. No other drama has been
more often recycled, reimagined, reinterpreted, or
rethought by successive generations of critics and
dramaturges.

Shakespeare's acolytes reinvented *Hamlet* by
masking the play's hero with all sorts of disguises,
reflecting their eras and their endlessly varying
interpretations of the drama. The vacillating Danish
prince has been variously cast as an oedipal English
son, a singing Indian rajah, a Japanese Noh noble, a
manly daughter, and an effeminate man played by
women. The script has been shortened to a speedy
15-minute performance, lengthened to a glacial four-
plus hours, and staged without Act 5 (no grave dig-
gers, Osric, or fencing match). Among its countless
venues, it was first played at sea on a sailing ship off
Sierra Leone in 1607. Thanks to its antiroyal edge,
the play has been reworked worldwide to protest
assorted *bêtes noires*, including Germany's corrupt
Kaiser Wilhelm, repressive Communist regimes
(Chinese, Czech, Polish), and greedy American
tycoons. It has even survived animation, ranging
from Spike TV's cutesy characters (all LEGOs) to
Disney's likeable *The Lion King* (a Hamlet named
Simba).

When it comes to business, the unprecedented uncertainty and volatility facing leaders today create turbulence as great as any that buffeted Hamlet. Companies must constantly monitor and massage how they do what they do to adjust to new technologies, new competitive threats, and ever-changing market conditions. They must continually rethink, discover new ways to expand their trove of "whats," and further exploit those they already possess. Otherwise, they will fall victim to more flexible, proactive rivals demanding "your money *and* your life."

The online giant Amazon.com is a company that has proven itself a business counterpart to Hamlet—without sharing his fate. Amazon reinvents itself over and over thanks to its intuitive ability to rethink and rearrange its "whats." Beginning as an online bookseller with no glimmer of profitability on the horizon, the enterprise headed by the flamboyant Jeff Bezos has reincarnated itself and the relevant sets of "whats" as a general retailer, an online marketer, a provider of distribution services, a fulfillment company, and a digital utility. These days, Amazon is at the heart of a high percentage of all online retail transactions, and Bezos himself calls it a software company.

A *summa cum laude* Princeton graduate in computer science with an outsize personality, Bezos was a senior vice president in a Wall Street hedge fund in 1994 when he stumbled across a statistic:

Traffic on the Internet was growing at 2,300 percent per year. "I'd never heard of anything growing
like that, and I started thinking of a business plan
that would make sense" to take advantage of it, he
recalled years later.

All those Net surfers would be ready to buy things
online, Bezos reasoned, and after researching
what he might sell them, he decided on books. The
rationale: Almost every book was electronically
catalogued already, making them easy to find and
buy, but there were so many titles that no single
bookstore could carry them all. An online store
could offer any book a reader might want. When an
order came in, the book could simply be retrieved
from a distributor's warehouse, skipping the time,
expense, trouble, and—most important—all the
"whats" of planning, opening, and managing stores
and all those associated with procuring, holding,
and distributing inventory.

Bezos's assumptions turned out to be fatally flawed.
He soon learned that the bookselling business was
slow, cumbersome, and unreliable. To get books
quickly at good prices and make sure his customers
had a positive experience, he would have to assemble the "whats" to control the transactions from
beginning to end, which meant opening his own
warehouses, hiring staff, and buying inventory. His
business model was turned upside down: To build
and stock the necessary warehouses, which cost

about $50 million apiece, he had to sell $2 billion in bonds. Bezos decided to go ahead, but he built in a long-range edge by focusing on the performance of his warehousing and distribution "whats." Amazon's warehouses were highly computerized, continuously upgraded, and amazingly efficient—just the thing for handling various contingencies should they appear.

And therein lies a prescriptive key to Amazon's success in managing its "whats." Bezos knew that the purpose of his warehouses, accomplishing the **Fulfill-Orders** "what" at a performance level that met or exceeded customer expectations, wouldn't change much if at all. But Amazon's basic "what," **Sell-Books**, still had to prove out. Therefore, how Amazon used its inventory and distribution resources would continue to evolve. So instead of investing in immediate perfection, Bezos invested in agility—the ability to adapt to change in a timely manner. His warehouses were built to accommodate unfolding "whats" and "hows."

Bezos's foresight didn't help much in the short run, when the bursting of the dot-com bubble and the ensuing recession halted Amazon's sales growth. He responded by rethinking his basic "what," branching away from books to push into general retailing. Amazon's goods eventually would include cameras, office products, clothing, sporting goods, gourmet food, and jewelry. Nor did Bezos's expansionary tendencies stop at the water's edge: In 1998, he launched operations first in Britain and then in Germany, followed by France and Japan in 2000. He invaded Canada in 2002.

What managers should remember, though, is that Bezos, like Howard Schultz at Starbucks, recognized a pivot point before it was apparent to others. Starbucks started out being about the coffee, but it quickly became about the customer experience in its stores. And by prioritizing the "whats" that contribute to customer experience (such as connect-to-Internet in stores, as mentioned in Chapter 3, "First—Identify the 'Whats' That Are Truly Valuable"), Starbucks added numerous products and services that contributed to the overall experience.

Similarly, Amazon began by selling all kinds of books, building trust and familiarity among its customers. In the recession, Jeff Bezos could easily have fallen into the "how" trap by focusing on ways to sell more books. Instead, he was savvy enough to recognize that his customers' positive experiences gave him the license to bring more products and services to their attention. By distilling what was most important to his customers, Bezos expanded their relationship with Amazon (and its brand, which is a key component of value) well beyond books. (Similarly, Nike branched well beyond shoes to offer all sorts of things that enabled customers to "just do" almost anything in Nike's branded clothing, hats, and other paraphernalia.)

The efficiency of Amazon's warehouses finally paid off after yet another software upgrade put Bezos in a whole new business. His superior understanding of his rethought distribution operation allowed him to perform the **Fulfill-Order** "what" for other merchants, including Toys 'R' Us, Borders, and Target. The efficiency of Amazon's warehouses saved those companies money even after paying commissions, and that revenue stream offset much of the interest Amazon was paying on its huge debt.

In addition, the cutting-edge technology opened the way to new initiatives in other areas, which Bezos developed by setting up a cluster of what he called "two-pizza teams." These were five- to eight-person groups of idea people who, as their name implied, could be fed with two large pizzas. Out of these groups came innovations such as customer discussion boards on each product page and software for playing music and videos on the site.

Yet another epiphany opened Amazon.com as an online market to all comers, including competitors. Bezos invited purveyors of both new and used goods to list their products for sale on his site, and all items in a category—new or used, from insiders and outsiders alike—were included on the same page. Same-page listings seemed suicidal to analysts and even to many Amazon staffers. Having substantially improved his **Distribute-Products** "what," was Bezos now going to risk his relationship with vendors by making them go head-to-head with cheaper used goods?

Bezos followed his instincts, knowing that his basic customer-satisfaction metric depended not on the status of the goods, but on providing more of what the customers wanted to buy. In the end, the idea became a key part of Amazon's strategy, opening up a new stream of revenue. The outside vendors paid commissions on sales of goods that Amazon never touched, producing almost pure profit for Bezos's company.

Amazon was also building brand and customer loyalty by making price comparisons easy. "Giving people the choice to buy new and used side by side is good for customers," Bezos said. "They're not going to hurt themselves with that choice. The data we have tell us that customers who buy used books from us go on to buy more new books than they have ever bought before." Some insurance companies offer this sort of side-by-side pricing as well, and even advertise it. But unlike Amazon, which actually helps a customer choose a product, the insurance companies are deliberately sending away customers they don't want because of their risk profiles. Not that that's a bad thing; it's just that a very similar-looking thing can be a very different "what" in reality.

The lesson here is that leaders need to be fully aware of their own roles and contributions to their value chains, as well as to customer and partner experiences. Bezos built up the Amazon brand first by moving beyond books and then beyond proprietary goods, making its basic "what" a buying experience (just as Starbucks centered its strategy around the café experience and not just coffee). The progression made it natural for Amazon to showcase goods from other suppliers, and customers found the expanded range of items useful and valuable. Any established Amazon vendors who resented the new competition had to weigh losing the Amazon business if they left in a huff. In the end, most of them stayed.

It's equally important to remain open to change. Many of the companies profiled in these pages have tested various assumptions and models on their way to success. Generally, experimentation ends with success, but not at Amazon. It never stops testing and trying out new ideas to keep expanding on its enormous achievements.

In fact, the same-page listings experiment led Bezos to another counterintuitive move: Amazon offered outsiders access to some of its proprietary information—the company's family jewels, its **Develop-Software** "what"—and let them use their insights to help build new service applications aligned with Amazon technology. The result was a vast expansion of the site's range of offerings. These days, some 200,000 outside Web developers are providing free help in building Amazon's core business. Scanbuy, for instance, lets people use their cell phones to compare retail-store prices with Amazon's online prices.

Still another moment of illumination in 2002 produced what became Amazon Web Services. Bezos came up with the idea of renting out parts of his company's complex infrastructure and expertise to smaller companies, which happily paid for services that would cost more to develop themselves. In effect, Amazon morphed into a digital utility by taking over some of its customers' "whats"—specifically, the management of some of their technology needs, along with the physical handling of assorted goods. Among Amazon's service offerings are the following:

- Elastic Compute Cloud (EC2), which rents out unused computer capacity on Amazon's thousands of servers. Most of the time, a large part of the capacity isn't needed and can easily be made available to others, adding yet another new income stream. EC2 prices to outsiders start at just 10 cents an hour for the equivalent of a basic server, an excellent deal for small start-ups trying to minimize capital investment.

One EC2 customer is Powerset, a much-touted upstart that aims to out-Google Google with a revolutionary new search engine. The engine was developed by just 22 staffers, and CEO Barney Pell says the Amazon service saved him $1 million on computer hardware and salaries for a gaggle of software writers. Using EC2 cut his first-year capital costs in half—and Powerset's search engine proved so successful that Microsoft soon snapped up the company for a price rumored (outside of Microsoft) to be $100 million.

- Simple Storage Service (S3), which provides data storage on Amazon devices. For only 15 cents per gigabyte per month, programmers and businesses can store data and software they don't want cluttering up their own disks. As of April 2007, S3 held fully 5 billion such "objects," or pieces of data.

SmugMug Inc., an online photo-sharing start-up, turned to S3 to back up all of its customers' photos. Chris MacAskill, SmugMug's cofounder and president, says the service saves the company $500,000 a year over the cost of buying its own storage devices. "Everything we can get Amazon to do, we will get Amazon to do," he says, adding: "You're going to see all kinds of start-ups get a much better and faster start" by using Amazon's services.

- Fulfillment by Amazon, which offers to perform **Store-Inventory** and **Fulfill-Order** "whats" for merchants anywhere. Amazon started its fulfillment business by handling orders for big companies, then broadened the offer to any merchants selling on Amazon.com. Now, any retailer anywhere can use one of Amazon's distribution centers, which have grown to number 20 worldwide. A total of 10 million square feet can be rented for about 45 cents per square foot per month.

Small and mid-size businesses looking to outsource their **Fulfill-Order** "what" have to ship their goods to the nearest Amazon distribution center, thus paying twice to get merchandise to their customers. But it's still a bargain in return for quick and flawless execution of orders, and the clients also benefit from the discounts Amazon gets from shipping companies. Above all, though, they save the time and labor of handling their own orders. "Usually, there's not enough hours in the week to ship everything," says Barry Mark, a dealer in surplus books who runs Treebeard Books from his home in Palm Beach County, Florida.

As with the selling of its excess technological power, renting out unneeded physical space is a boon for Amazon. Besides bringing in extra revenue, the superb management of its warehouse and distribution "whats" makes use of space that will probably be needed for Amazon's own growth in the long run but would be lying fallow if not for the outside clients. It's classic "how"-trap thinking that an organization needs to invest to grow, accepting that there will be surplus until the growth is realized. Amazon has figured out how to ensure that it can grow if need be while turning its investment into a source of revenue until that growth comes. But if the industry or the economy contracts in the meantime, a solid model is in place to allow others to make use of additional resources that become available.

Amazon's Web Services extract revenue from "whats" designed for a peak capacity that Amazon hardly ever needs. "We have this beautiful, elegant, high-IQ part of our business that we have been working hard on for many years," Bezos explains. "We've gotten good at it. Why not make money off it another way?" Some argue that he is passing up moneymaking opportunities by charging so little for his services. But that, he says, is part of Amazon's basic strategy: "There are two kinds of companies: those that try to charge more and those that work to charge less. We will be the second."

Another of Amazon's Web Services, and possibly its most intriguing, is one that uses human intelligence to perform chores computers aren't good at doing. Amazon Mechanical Turk (MTurk) had its origins in 2004, when the company was trying to match photos with the entries in an online Yellow Pages directory containing thousands of businesses. People can easily recognize and match images, but computers can't, so Amazon set up a Web site, mturk.com, that pays anyone willing to sort them. The name pays ironic homage to an 18th-century hoax, a chess-playing automaton dubbed "The Turk" that actually had a human chess master hidden inside.

Amazon's wages for this service were also counterintuitive: It offered just a penny or two per photo. Surprisingly, photo sorters showed up in droves. Since then, dozens of companies have used thousands of volunteer "Turkers" to do HITs, or human intelligence tasks—odd jobs ranging from transcribing Podcast segments to retouching photos for Web sites. Turkers are still paid a pittance for the work. Most seem to do it as a diversion, akin to filling in crossword puzzles, and they count their wages as pin money. Critics have carped that the billionaire Bezos has created a virtual sweatshop. But Mitch Fernandez, a disabled former U.S. Army linguist, told *The New York Times* that he used Turking as a form of therapy to reintroduce him to work. He said he could earn $100 a week by being a Turker for two hours a day and had made $4,000 in nine months.

MTurk is a version of so-called crowd-sourcing, in which practitioners tap the collective mind of the Web. But Bezos calls it "artificial artificial intelligence," and Amazon collects 10 percent of the cost of every HIT that is successfully completed for a client. MTurk is yet another example of how the smartest rethinkers focus on the outcome—the "what"—making "how" it gets done a second-order question. As Bezos certainly recognized, the best solution to the problem at hand was also the simplest and cheapest. You can't ask for anything better than that.

Some venture capitalists have started urging their start-up clients to take advantage of Amazon's various offerings to save money and get to market faster. "They're taking their store in the sky and unbundling it," said Peter Rip, a general partner in Crosslink Capital. But Bezos thinks the services will appeal to businesses of all sizes, and he already has some big-name clients to prove the point. Microsoft, for instance, uses S3 to speed up software downloads, and Linden Lab uses it to support its fast-growing Second Life online virtual world.

And Jeff Bezos is not finished yet. His eye is trained on the race to build an even bigger "what," the platform for the Web of the future, the underlying layer of basic services supporting individual Web sites. Now, says Tim O'Reilly, an Internet pundit and CEO of tech publisher O'Reilly Media, "Amazon's a pretty serious dark horse. Jeff really understands that if he doesn't become a platform player, he's at the mercy of those who do."

Amazon's Unbox and MP3 services already let customers download videos and music. But its new-new thing, the Kindle electronic book reader, is being hailed as a revolution in the way readers read, writers write, and publishers publish. With Kindle, Amazon can be said to be returning to its roots. It may also be preparing for another incarnation.

Bezos calls Kindle "the most important thing we've ever done," and that pronouncement shouldn't be shrugged off as just another bit of Bezos hype. The book-size, book-weight device can be held in one's lap or read from while curled up in bed. Its screen and text so resemble a book that a user can sink, without distraction, into the familiar trance of reading. Best of all, Kindle wirelessly enables a reader to choose, buy, and download a book, all within a minute. The device itself can hold a small library of 200 books, and a memory card can add hundreds more. You can also subscribe to newspapers, magazines, and blogs via Kindle; search text for names, words, and phrases; even highlight passages. The device's rechargeable battery is good for 30 hours of reading, and its text size can be made larger or smaller to suit the needs of the reader.

Kindle isn't perfect. Costing $399 and offering best-selling books for $9.99 apiece puts it on the pricey side. You have to be careful not to drop it, and taking it to the beach could be risky. Text shows up as black on white only; passages can't be copied, printed, or e-mailed; and books for Kindle are available only from Amazon. But, promises Bezos, Kindle can get a reader any book ever printed in less than a minute's time.

The key "what" for Amazon, however, is that Kindle is an Internet device perpetually connected by a cell-phone broadband service that works almost everywhere. Stock analyst Scott Devitt, of Stifel, Nicolaus & Company, thinks this could do much more than re-create the business of e-books. "With time, we believe Amazon Kindle could be Amazon. com's Trojan Horse into a complete 'always-on' connection to all Amazon offerings," he says. If Devitt is right, dark-horse Amazon would take a solid lead in the race against Google and Microsoft to build the Web platform of the future.

Amazon's amazing capacity for rethinking and rearranging its "whats" and reimagining its "hows" epitomizes today's successful businesses. But the bookseller-cum-general retailer, fulfillment company, digital utility, and so on, is not alone. Another company practiced in the art of reincarnation is Procter & Gamble. The storied old household-products maker has rethought its innovation "whats" to create and re-create branded products that, in the words of its statement of purpose, provide "superior quality and value that improves the lives of the world's consumers." It is no small feat that P&G has figured out how to maintain market position in a world that refuses to stand still.

P&G SOARS BY MORPHING ITS INNOVATION "WHATS"

In 1999, when A.G. Lafley was named chief executive of the Procter & Gamble Company, sales and earnings were shrinking. After supplying consumers with a seemingly endless supply of new products and services for 162 years, the company was running out of ideas. To his credit, Lafley realized that new technologies and new competitors had speeded up the pace of business while globalization had fragmented its processes and procedures. To stay in the race, P&G had to churn out innovations much faster but without jeopardizing profitability. In other words, it had to rethink. Success in managing its **Innovate-Product** "what" would be central to the company's very survival.

At the time, P&G was getting barely 10 percent of its product ideas from outsiders. But Lafley instinctively knew that his company could no longer go it alone. After all, no one company has been given a monopoly on good ideas. Frequent communication with outside innovators, customers, suppliers, and internal experts is vital. "We don't care where the ideas come from," said Lafley, decreeing that, henceforth, P&G would work to source 50 percent of its **Create-New-Product** ideas from outside the company. The flip side was that the company did care about the "whats" downstream from the ideas—namely design, prototype, manufacture, market, and sell-products.

Nabil Y. Sakkab, senior vice president for corporate research and development, says experience shows that 1,000 ideas must be filtered to find one "big idea," the kind that will return, say, $100 million of new business. So to create $4 billion of new business, the goal Lafley had laid out, P&G would have had to access and vet 40,000 ideas, an impossibility under the old regimen given "how" they went about it. Remaking the insular manufacturing company's culture and opening it up to fresh ideas became a necessity.

To get things started, Lafley rethought P&G's **Research-and-Develop-Product** "whats" by reframing them as "connect and develop," or C&D. That seemingly small change in terminology set product developers and marketing people to thinking about their jobs in a new way. No longer were they to be hidden away in their research labs, creating and inventing in solitude. The new mind-set was outward-looking, and it encompassed an estimated 1.5 million innovators around the world who could help P&G solve problems and think up ideas for new products. Alliances were no longer part of the company's strategy; they *were* its strategy, making a previously unimportant "what," **Manage-Partner-Relationships**, crucial to P&G.

Now the burning question became: How do we connect with all these brilliant minds? How do we get them to come forward with their ideas and help the company achieve success? With the new emphasis on collaboration and connectivity, the answer was technology.

Within P&G, there are 22 so-called communities of practice. Self-organizing and self-led, these groups keep the company on the leading edge of emerging technologies and disseminate pertinent pieces of internal knowledge throughout the company, thereby ensuring that every product brand can take advantage of breakthrough ideas and events that emerge in another bailiwick. The company moved to supplement its intranet with external links and smart reporting systems to create a virtual "global lunchroom." It went in search of new-product ideas at stables of talent like NineSigma and InnoCentive.

And it began building its own infrastructure, including its YourEncore network, a joint venture with Eli Lilly that utilizes retired scientists and engineers, and the Technology Entrepreneurs Network of 75 innovation seekers located in the far reaches of the world. The Entrepreneurs Network is credited with identifying 10,000 products, product ideas, and promising technologies.

From the outset, P&G wanted its internal idea creators to understand that it wasn't outsourcing R&D but, rather, in-sourcing innovation. Maintaining **Evaluate-Innovation** as an internal "what" is crucial, the company believes. Otherwise, you lose the ability to judge the value of what you are connecting to. To convince employees that it wasn't looking to substitute low-cost external talent for higher-cost internal know-how, P&G stressed that what it really wanted was a "turbo-charged" R&D operation with great scientists and facilities and with a changed culture that rewarded people for bringing concepts in from outside as well as for creating from the inside.

And, just as it promised, P&G has not shrunk its internal R&D workforce. Rather, it has used it to judge the promise and value of what comes in from outside. Going forward, the company hopes to develop more of a co-invention relationship with its outside resources as opposed to a transaction-based one. After surveying the business landscape for areas offering the most valuable opportunities, P&G will broadcast its assessment to the world, find someone who has a solution, and then collaborate internally and externally to fine-tune the resulting product.

After that, it becomes all about execution. And, as Sakkab cautions, once you've made a connection and taken the time to polish it, you have to make clear who will own which piece of the work. In other words, you have to effectively manage your **Innovate-New-Products** "what."

But for all the marvels of technology, P&G, whose brands touch the lives of people around the world 3 billion times a day, has learned that it cannot successfully create solutions to satisfy consumer needs and fix customer problems without first gaining a deep understanding of what those diverse needs and wants are by means of the **Research-Market-Trends** "what." And the best way to do that is through firsthand experience gained by spending time with consumers in their homes and workplaces, developing a sense of how they live and what kinds of products and services would make their lives better. It's what some people call "social anthropology."

The most valuable insights are those that lead a C&D leader to consumers' unarticulated needs. But, as Sakkab points out, "You don't discover an unarticulated need by talking to a consumer; you discover it by observing a consumer." Sakkab estimates that he himself has been in about a thousand consumer

homes all over the world. He has observed people—
both rich and poor—doing dishes, washing floors,
and laundering diapers in China, Brazil, and elsewhere. That P&G has finely honed its "what" for
discovering consumers' real need is proved by its
ownership of the number one or number two brand
in more than 20 different consumer categories.

Five years after Lafley's groundbreaking directive,
innovating innovation had notably increased the efficiency of the company's R&D investments. In fact,
P&G's innovation success rate had doubled, and
when translated to the income statement, the new-
found efficiency looked like this: a 19 percent jump in
2004 sales and a 25 percent rise in earnings, a remark-
able achievement for a company of P&G's size.

Today, P&G has regained its cherished spot as the
most innovative packaged-goods marketer. Thanks
largely to rethinking and ideas generated from outside its once-impenetrable walls, the company has
won some 27,000 patents, while 23 of its quality
leadership brands have met its benchmark for success by reaching or exceeding $1 billion in annual
sales. C&D productivity is up by 60 percent and
innovation success rates, as measured by projects
meeting financial criteria, hover around 70 percent.
These achievements helped the company report six
consecutive years of double-digit profit growth. All
of this is a testament to Procter & Gamble's mastery of **Manage-Talent** "whats" and to A.G. Lafley's
innovative idea for innovating innovation.

As for the future, it's all about how a company manages co-creation. What used to be "solely our job," Sakkab says, is now "everybody's job." And it's every company's job to rethink and manage its innovation capability in ways that maximize the enormous talent available just for the asking.

The rethinking you have encountered in this book demonstrates wide-ranging mastery by a diverse group of businesses with an amazingly varied complement of "whats." Their stories suggest the overwhelming and sometimes confusing array of options you confront today in managing your own business. I hope these accounts help you identify, analyze, and understand your "whats" as you rethink and go forth to best your competition.

If you succeed, you'll discover a whole new way of looking at your own business and at business in general. You will be liberated from the blinder-like tunnel vision of a narrow focus on costs, procedures, sequencing, and all the other "hows" of the game. Quite suddenly, you will be soaring above the business terrain with a bird's-eye view of the "whats" that are important and an understanding of why they fit together. You will be in control of your world in a way you have never experienced.

Rethinking will set you free.

Key Concepts

PREVIOUS METHODS FOR business improvement largely have been about optimization and improvement, and many of them have been very successful in helping people achieve dramatic, even revolutionary improvements. However, there hasn't been a lens that not only enables, but encourages people to rethink not just their own work, but their entire operating model in their business ecosystem. That is why we have turned our focus to looking at "what" the work is before asking "how" it should be performed. I've included this concepts section as a useful quick reference to the basic ideas in this book to help you in your rethinking journey.

CONVENTIONAL "HOW" BUSINESS VIEWS

For much of the past century, people have looked at organizations through one of two lenses: a people view (the organization chart) or a financial view (spreadsheets, reports, profit and loss tables, and so forth). These are "how" views of the organization, in terms of "how" they currently are structured and organized, and "how" funds are budgeted and spent. Although these are valid tools and remain vital, they are often used in a way that limits the view of the person to the inside of the four walls of the organization. In today's increasingly complex ecosystems of customer and partner relationships, those inward-facing views are insufficient. These views are rarely a good place to start when rethinking.

Process views can often traverse the artificial boundaries that are sometimes implied or created with the workflow view. Figure 1 is a good example of a common workflow process map. Process maps are a valuable way to capture the specific steps of how the work is performed, and they can also be useful for describing past or future state work flow. There are no real rules for creating a process map (which is an asset in the flexibility it provides, as well as a risk in the sense that it can be difficult to know if the map is complete and accurate), and they are typically a collection of iconic shapes, lines, and arrows. The following "how" map is for a

Create-Insurance-Quote "what" discussed in Chapter 1, "How the 'How' Trap Is Trapping You."

Think of Create-Insurance-Quote as a three dimensional box. As long as the outcome of achieving that "what" is accomplished, "how" the work is done in terms of steps of work, the people doing the work, the technology, and so forth can be done any number of ways. Figure 1 is just one way of representing the work flow. The number of steps can change, the shapes and labels can change in terms of "how" the work is done, but the label of the "what" is still Create-Insurance-quote, and that's the key distinction in the book—there is a relationship between what the work is and how it is performed. However, you can change "how" it is done, without changing "what" is being done (you could outsource it, to use a very simple example).

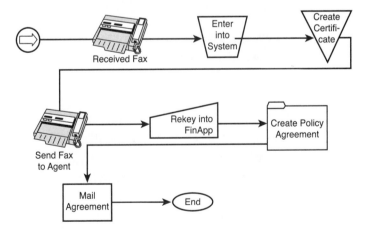

Figure 1: Common workflow process map

When talking to people about their work requirements, a process map is commonly presented as
the current state of the work (although past and
future state maps are also common). If people often
assume that the map reflects the current state and
all or most of the current requirements are being
met, then it is very easy to fall into a "how" trap
here and assume that this is a good starting point
for requirements analysis in this instance. Starting with a "how" view, and then describing a different "how" view is very difficult. It is much easier
to look at the "how," then understand the "what" it
is connected to. Once that "what" is understood,
the discussion of whether this is the best "how" or
which parts of the "how" to change becomes much
simpler.

There are a number of things worth pointing out in
this representative process map in Figure 1:

- **Where does the arrow at the top left
  part of the page come from?** Clearly
  that is the start of the process, but
  what causes it to start? Where does it
  sit relative to other processes? What
  is the parent process? Are there other
  child processes? All of these things
  are attributes that can be captured in
  a disciplined way and attached to the
  "what."

- **Is the "Send Fax" step a requirement or not?** More than likely the requirement is to **Communicate-Status**, as that is really "what" is being done, and the fax machine is more "how" it is currently being done. Now that's not to say that it couldn't be required either through some regulation or customer contract that a fax machine has to be used—while it is unlikely, it's not clear from the process map. This is a very good example of where talking with a subject matter expert can blur the line between what is truly required and what is simply a matter of how the work is being done today. Classic "how" trap.

- **Who is the "customer" of this work?** Someone is clearly benefitting from this work—an insurance customer and/or the insurance agent preparing the quote. What performance expectations have been set? Should this take five minutes, a day, or a week? Do they expect it to be free? What level of quality do they expect? How close to the final price must it be? Does the insurance quote created here need to comply with some specific regulation? These are important questions that are not explicitly captured in the map, which are also attributes to associate with the "what."

- **Is some of this work already outsourced?** The box labeled "Mail Agreement" is something that could easily be performed by a third-party fulfillment house, as that is very common. While there's nothing wrong with that, if someone wants to make a change to people, or process, or the supporting technology, they may not be able to; and if they are able to, there may be a very different set of security, technology, and other requirements that are not obvious from this process map.

- **What is the value of this work to the department, the division, or the organization as a whole? Is this a core function or a commodity function?** Maybe creating insurance quotes are the one reason their customers do business with them, and maybe it's generic across the industry and no one really pays any attention to it (like the airport check-in example discussed in Chapter 1). If someone in the information technology department is talking about adding some software to automate this work, and they don't know it's a primary source of differentiation, there's a great deal of risk there—just as if someone were looking to improve the process workflow and it is a commodity function. (Like airport check-in, as a commodity function, no one should care who does it, or what the process or what technology supports it, as long as the correct outcome is achieved). This is covered in greater length in Chapter 3, "First—Identify the 'Whats' That Are Truly Valuable."

- **How is it currently performing?** Chapter 4, "Second—Know What You Are (and Aren't) Good At," talks about value and performance as two of the key places to start rethinking. This amounts to assigning explicit performance expectations to work, and ensuring that there is some link—at least assertion based, if not proven—to indicate whether the work is a direct cause of the good or bad performance of the organization as a whole.

WHAT IS, AND IS NOT, A "WHAT"

A great example of why managers should appreciate the importance of understanding the "whats" of the work separated from their "hows" is the basic employee performance evaluation. Managers need to set specific outcome targets for each employee, and in most cases the manager shouldn't care "how" they go about it as long as it's legal and within budgetary constraints. Unfortunately, most employee targets are tied to a set of goals (like a scorecard) that are connected to a "how" view of people, or process, which makes it very difficult to assert and test the real value/performance drivers discussed in Chapters 3 and 4. As a consequence, there's a risk that organizations are not focusing their cost cutting, or innovation, or customer satisfaction, or what-have-you initiatives on the right things. My work has shown that this is almost always the case to some degree.

At this point I will take a slightly more grammatical perspective in pointing out that a key difference between a "what" and "how" lies in the verbs used to name them. Notice in the following list that the "whats" have verbs that are outcome verbs. In the first one, what you are doing is acquiring customers, and the example "how" to the right is using the telephone. There are many other "hows" that can be used to acquire customers, whether it's going to a trade show or e-mailing a list of prospective customers that was purchased from a third party. The point is, define the "what" outcome that you need to be doing, and then get into the conversation of "how" to do it.

What	How
Acquire-New-Customers	Phone prospects
Deliver-Product	Truck product to customer
Create-Purchase-Order	Complete order form document
Generate-Invoices	Run invoicing reporting program
Pay-Employee	Transmit funds to third-party payroll company

READING A HEAT MAP

Heat maps are a very powerful way of representing "whats" and their relationships to one another. Adding color or "heat" helps inform conversations about the "whats" that are most in need of attention. The colors added to the heat maps reflect the scores linked to responses to questions I ask people at all levels in an organization about performance, value, predictability, connectedness, compliance, and others. The following is a quick review on those terms:

1. Business Value (Chapter 3)

   - How strongly does it connect to the performance of a key performance indicator of the organization?

   - Is it part of the brand or identity relative to why customers, partners, or employees work with you?

   - How useful or valuable would it be to invest in improving the performance?

2. Performance (Chapter 4)

   - How is it currently performing today?

   - Do we know and understand what causes performance today?

   - Do we know and understand what it would take to improve performance?

3. Connectedness (Chapter 5)

   - How standalone is the work versus heavily interconnected to other work?

   - Is some or all of the work outsourced (do we control it)?

   - Does the "what" interact with organizations across the "corporate" boundary?

4. Predictability/Maturity (Chapter 6)

- How predictable is the outcome/
  output of the work?

- How finite, common, and known are
  the things that cause the outcome/
  output to vary?

- How much do we control the inputs to
  the work?

5. Compliance (Chapter 7)
  This one is a little unusual because you
  will often want to ask these questions for
  each regulation and policy whether you
  are looking for all regulations/policies
  that touch a single area of work, or you
  are looking at a single regulation/policy
  that touches multiple areas of work.

- What is the regulation (law) or policy
  (internal) that is linked to this work?

- How many regulations or policies are
  linked to this work?

- If known, is the work in compliance
  with the regulations or policies?

The book provides some guidance about how to
score the answers to these questions, and I typically
score with equal weighting to each question and try
to keep the answers to Yes/No and High, Medium,
and Low.

Figure 2 shows a parent "what" that consists of five child "whats" with various combinations of performance and business value ratings. (Note: This is a simplistic heat map example. Because the book is printed in black & white, you cannot see the colors. For more examples, which are in color, please go to www.rethinkbook.com.) Something that's quite common in interviewing individuals is that they have a very specific set of ideas about what is the most important thing that should be done to improve things. However, when the discussion lacks the discipline and rigor of objectively defined work such as "whats," it can be hard to know if that person's suggestion makes the most sense.

For example, **Prepare-Quote** is a "what" child in the **Develop-Opportunity** example in Figure 2. If someone said that automating the **Prepare-Quote** "what" is the most important thing to do, with this diagram you now have some information to respond to that person. Because the **Develop-Opportunity** "what" is high value and performing poorly, it makes sense to talk about improving its performance. Then the conversation should be, do we know or have assertions about which of the child capabilities cause the parent to perform the way it does. The **Assess-Customer-Needs** "what" is high value but it's already performing well, so that might not be the first place to look to improve the performance of the parent and continue the conversation from there. Based on this information, however, the

Prepare-Quote "what" is performing Medium and it's also Medium business value. So just looking at business value and performance, we would have to gather some additional information to justify a conclusion to proceed with a discussion about investing time, money, or energy in that particular "what." The accomplishment here is that instead of simply arguing opinions about whether **Prepare-Quote** is a "what" that needs to be automated (which is a "how" decision), you are able to have a more objective discussion and say that there needs to be a more compelling business case for doing anything to **Prepare-Quote**, rather than having any conversation about whether the right "how" change is to automate it.

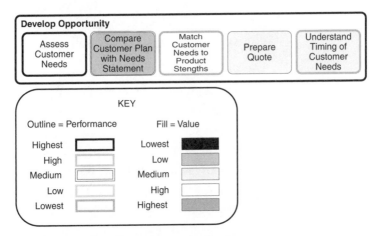

Figure 2: Develop opportunity heat map

GETTING TO THE LIST OF "WHATS"

The list of "whats" isn't simply a list. The list reflects relationships that are described as levels, where a Level 1 map, or list, is made up of the highest level "whats" that make up an organization. Each "what" in Level 1 is made up of several more specific "whats" that are the Level 2 "whats," and Level 2 is then made up of the Level 3 "whats" and so on, often going down five to seven levels deep. People often ask what the "right" depth is, and my experience has been that it first depends on the following:

- What questions are you asking in terms of what opportunities you are looking to address, or which problems you are looking to solve? Some issues are higher level issues than others, so in some cases there is no value in going several levels deep.

- Who are you talking to? If you are talking with someone in the shipping dock, that's a pretty specific set of "whats," and it's likely that the person doing that work will be talking about "whats" that may be at levels, four, five, and six. By contrast, if you are talking to a senior executive, she won't be talking at the same level of detail as the person in the shipping dock, so in those cases, it's likely that Levels 1-4 are likely places for the conversation to focus.

- Apart from any specific instructions you
  get from a manual or book, you need
  to let value guide you in decisions like
  this. If you are talking with the shipping
  dock about a "what" such as **Confirm-
  Shipment-Complete**, depending on the
  purpose of your efforts, that may be too
  detailed, or it may not be detailed enough.
  The more you do this work, the better you
  will become at making these decisions.

Figure 3 is a common representation of a Level 1
map, where the inside shapes, numbered 1-5 are
the "whats" that make up the business—these
labels will vary somewhat across industries, but not
much. Government organizations, schools, health-
care organizations, and some particularly unusual
industries such as Oil and Gas—because of what
they call "upstream" and "downstream"—will also
make Level 1 look different. In the retail industry,
they don't really develop products and services,
so that "what" #1 would be planning and procure-
ment for the items that they sell. A key point is that
there isn't a canonical list of "whats." If people want
to organize their "whats" differently, that's okay—
the "whats" are by definition defined objectively,
and placement of the "whats" is a decision you can
make.

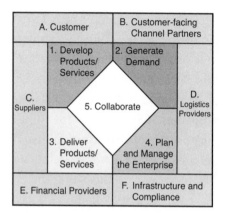

Figure 3: Level 1 map

On the outside of this particular Level 1 map, you will see items lettered A-F, which are the outside organizations that the business needs to interact with. A key point to make here is that the "whats" that make up the business are relatively stable and durable. A company might outsource all of its **Deliver-Products** "what" to UPS, like Toshiba did in Chapter 1. Even though another company is doing that "what," it's still part of the business. We talked about this with the Newman's Own company—even though there are a tiny number of employees in the company, it's still part of a very large business that includes several other companies that they outsource to. So the business is stable and durable, and it's up to each company to decide which of the "whats" in the business they want to perform.

A BIT MORE ABOUT LEVEL 1 MAPS

It is very common for an organization to be made up of several businesses, as represented in Figure 4. Some automotive companies have a different division for each different label, while other companies have divisions that do very different things. Nokia is a company that makes automotive tires and cellular phones. In those larger enterprises, there is an overall umbrella parent company, but each division should be viewed as its own business. One of the things very common in these businesses in the enterprise is that they come up with very specialized terms and labels for how they do their work. Because these businesses often don't communicate much with one another, it is almost as though they are speaking different languages. One of the big benefits of the "what" lens is that it helps to cut through these foreign languages and helps expose when the same "whats" exist. This opens the door to discussions about best-practice "hows" that can be used, or even whether it makes sense for each division to be doing the same "whats" in specific cases. The Zip code example in Chapter 1 is a vivid illustration of how much money can be saved very quickly using this approach.

An Enterprise Is a Legal Entity That Can Be Made Up of Many Separate Businesses

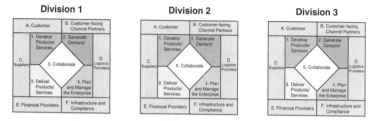

When looking at how capability maps are implemented, in terms of people, IT, processes, it becomes evident where:

1. The same capability is being performed by the same people
2. The same capability is not being implemented the same way

Figure 4: An organization made up of several businesses

LEVEL 2 MAPS

As I mentioned before, the "whats" in Level 2 are the "whats" that are inside of each Level 1 "what," the so-called children of each Level 1 parent. So, if you see below in the Level 1 "what" called **Generate-Demand**, the children of **Generate-Demand**, are the Level 2 "whats" that are **Manage-Partner-Relationships**, **Market-Products**, and **Sell-Products**.

When you get into Level 2, the first parent/child relationships emerge. Numbering the "whats" makes it easier to refer to individual "whats," and the numbering helps to reinforce the notion of the parent/ child hierarchy. Again, there is no right or wrong way to organize these relationships. Some people would have ten Level 2 "whats" in the **Generate-Demand** "what" whereas others would prefer to see that level of detail in Level 2.

1.0 Create-Products/Services

  1.1 Develop-New-Product/Service-Concepts-and-Plans

  1.2 Design-New-Product/Service-and-Processes

  1.3 Develop-New-Products/Services

  1.4 Launch-Products/services

  1.5 Manage-Existing-Products/Services-(Manage-Product/Service-Lifecycle)

  1.6 Withdraw-Existing-Product/Service

2.0 Generate-Demand

  2.1 Manage-Partner-Relationships

  2.2 Market-Products/Services

  2.3 Sell-Products/Services

3.0 Deliver-Products

  3.1 Plan-Long-Term-Fulfillment

  3.2 Procure-Raw-Materials

  3.3 Produce-Product

3.4   Deliver-Services

3.5   Ship-Product

3.6   Maintain-Business-Intelligence

4.0 Plan-and-Manage-the-Business

4.1   Complete-Strategic-Planning

4.2   Manage-Capital

4.3   Manage-Culture-and-Corporate-Values

4.4   Manage-Finances

4.5   Manage-Projects

4.6   Manage-Human-Resources

4.7   Manage-Compliance-and-Risk

4.8   Manage-IT-Services

5.0 Manage-Collaboration

5.1   Manage-Strategy

5.2   Manage-Cross-Group-Planning

5.3   Manage-Operations

This is Level 2, and although it is tempting to show Level 3, the template list expands to more than 200 in Level 3, and then more than 1,000 at Level 4. So instead of just listing them here, that information is available at www.rethinkbook.com.

Hopefully you will be able to make good use of this Key Concepts section in your rethinking endeavors.

Index

A

A350 jet (Airbus), 98
A380 jet (Airbus), 96
ACSI (American Customer
    Satisfaction Index), 9
Adam Aircraft, 148-149
airline industry
    Airbus
        A350 jet, 98
        A380 jet, 96
    Boeing 787 Dreamliner, 93-99
    Eclipse, 134
    flight check-in procedures, 17-18
    JetBlue, 99-105
Alcoa, 41-48, 57
Alenia Aeronautica, 99
Alexander, Whit, 150, 152, 154, 166,
    167. *See also* Cranium
All Nippon Airways, 98

Amazon.com, 106, 163, 169-186
    Amazon Web Services, 178-183
        *Amazon Mechanical Turk
            (MTurk), 182-183*
        *Elastic Compute Cloud (EC2),
            178-179*
        Fulfillment by Amazon, 180
        *Simple Storage Service
            (S3), 179*
    Develop-Software "what,"
177-178
        Distribute-Products "what,"
        176-177
        Fulfill-Orders "what," 173
        Fulfill-Order "what," 175
        Kindle, 184-185
        Sell-Books "what," 173-174
    Amazon Mechanical Turk
        (MTurk), 182-183

Amazon Web Services, 178-183
    Amazon Mechanical Turk
      (MTurk), 182-183
    Elastic Compute Cloud (EC2),
      178-179
    Fulfillment by Amazon, 180
    Simple Storage Service (S3), 179
American Customer Satisfaction
    Index (ACSI), 9
analysis, units of
    departments, 32-33
    processes, 33-34
    tasks, 28-30
    "whats," 34-38
    workers, 31
Analyze-Gamer-Interaction "what"
    (Cranium), 156
Analyze-Gamer-Reaction "what"
    (Cranium), 156, 161
Apply-Safety-Clothing "what"
    (Alcoa), 42
Arizona Diamondbacks' stadium,
    redecoration of, 65
Assemble-Fire-Extinguisher
    "what" (Eclipse Aviation
    Corporation), 146
Assemble-Instrument-Panel
    "what" (Eclipse Aviation
    Corporation), 145
Assign-Qualified-Resource-to-Task
    "what" (Alcoa), 42
Automation (Diebold), 32

B

Balloon Lagoon, 161
Barnes & Noble, 163
Bell, James, 98

Berra, Lawrence Peter "Yogi," 27
Beyond Paycheck to Paycheck!
    (Rubin), 129
Bezos, Jeff, 169-186. *See also*
    Amazon.com
Bigger, Thomas J., 85
bin Laden, Osama, 110
Boeing, 93-99
Bowery Savings Bank of New
    York, 32
Bradbury, Ray, 91
Brokaw, Tom, 93
Buffett, Warren, 39
Burgerville, 66-71
Bush, George W., 43, 111
business capabilities. *See* "whats"
business value
    definition of, 40
    evaluating, 202
BuzzMachine, 80

C

Calhoun, Jack, 5
Calloway, Bertha, 117
capabilities. *See* "whats"
Cessna, 148
Champy, James, 34
check-in procedures (airlines), 17-18
CHIFF (clever, high quality,
    innovative, friendly, fun), 166
Chrysler, 92
Clark, Richard T., 87
Cochran, Jacques, 133
compliance, 110
    analyzing legal status of "whats,"
      114-116
    evaluating, 203

importance and impact on business, 112-114

Intrade case study, 110-114

matching laws and "whats," 114-115

Confirm-Safe-Work-Environment "what" (Alcoa), 42

connectedness
Dell case study, 78-82
evaluating, 202
importance and impact of connections, 88-90
Merck & Company case study, 82-87

Connect-Skin-to-Skeleton "what" (Eclipse Aviation Corporation), 143-145

Connect-to-Internet "what" (Alcoa), 57-58

conventional "how" business views, 194-199

Cooper, Anderson, 102

Country Natural Beef, 68

Cranium Cadoo, 159

Cranium, 152-167
Analyze-Gamer-Interaction "what," 156
Analyze-Gamer-Reaction "what," 156, 161
Create-New-Game "what," 154-160
Create-Prototype "what," 156
Distribute-Product "what," 162-164
Generate-Demand "what," 163-165

Manage-Partner-Relationships "what," 165
overview, 152-153
Recruit-New-Talent "what," 165-166
Sell-Game "what," 164
success and accomplishments, 167-168
Test-Prototype "what," 156

Create-Insurance-Quote "what," 195-199

Create-New-Customer "what" (Amazon.com), 106

Create-New-Game "what" (Cranium), 154-160

Create-New-Product "what"
Eclipse Aviation Corporation case study, 144
ING DIRECT case study, 127
Newman's Own case study, 54
P & G (Procter & Gamble) case study, 187

Create-Prototype "what" (Cranium), 156

CRM (customer relationship management) software, 2

Crosslink Capital, 183

Customer Bill of Rights (JetBlue), 102

customer relationship management (CRM) software, 2

D

D'Angelo, Anthony J., 151

Darwin, Charles, 7

Dayton Commercial Interiors, 64

Delaney, John, 110
Deliver-Product "what"
    Domino's Pizza case study, 59
    ING DIRECT case study, 123
Dell, 78-82
Dell, Michael, 78, 80
departments as units of analysis,
    32-33
Develop-Product "what" (Hon Hai
    Precision Industry), 73
Develop-Software "what"
    (Amazon.com), 177-178
Devitt, Scott, 185
Diebold, John, 32
Disclose-Financial-Data "what," 113
Dispose-Waste "what"
    (Burgerville), 67-69
Distribute-Products "what"
    Amazon.com case study, 176-177
    Cranium case study, 162-164
    Newman's Own case study, 53
Domino's Pizza, 59
Dreamliner (Boeing), 93-99

E

EC2 (Elastic Compute Cloud),
    178-179
Eclipseaviation.com, 147
Eclipse Aviation Corporation,
    134-149
    Assemble-Fire-Extinguisher
        "what," 146
    Assemble-Instrument-Panel
        "what," 145
    Connect-Skin-to-Skeleton
        "what," 143, 145

Create-New-Product
    "what," 144
Fabricate-Tail-Assembly
    "what," 142
Install-Toilet "what," 140
Manufacture-Product "what,"
    138-139, 142-144
overview, 134-137
success and accomplishments,
    149-150
Train-New-Pilot "what," 146
transparency, 147-149
Egometrics, 138
Elastic Compute Cloud (EC2),
    178-179
Eli Lilly, 189
Embraer, 148
Enron, 112
EPA (Environmental Protection
    Agency), 114-115
ERP (enterprise resource planning)
    software, 2, 34, 72
escaping "how" trap. See "how"
    trap, escaping
ETIRC Aviation, 148
Evaluate-Innovation "what"
    (Procter & Gamble), 189
evaluating performance. See
    performance

F

Fabricate-Tail-Assembly
    "what" (Eclipse Aviation
    Corporation), 142

Fernandez, Mitch, 182
flight check-in procedures, 17-18
Foodservice Consultants
  Society International Trendsetter
  Award, 70
Forrest, Andy, 158-160
Fosamax, 84
Fosbury, Dick, 12
Fosbury Flop, 12
Franz Bakery, 68
Fulfill-Demand "what" (ING
  DIRECT), 125
Fulfillment by Amazon, 180
Fulfill-Order "what"
  Amazon.com case study, 173-175
  Domino's Pizza example, 59

G

Gardner, Howard, 154-155
General Agreement on Trade in
  Services, 113
Generate-Demand "what"
  Cranium case study, 163-165
  ING DIRECT case study, 122
  Newman's Own case study, 53
Gilmartin, Raymond V., 82, 84
Goldwyn, Samuel, 77
Gore, Al, 164
Gou, Terry, 71-73
government regulations,
  compliance with. See compliance
Graves, Michael, 64

H

Hamlet (Shakespeare), 170
Hammer, Michael, 34
Hasbro, 166

heat maps
  example, 204-205
  reading, 201-205
high jump, Fosbury Flop, 12
high-value "whats," 40
Hole in the Wall Camps, 55
Home Depot, 8-10
Honda Motors, 148
Hon Hai Precision Industry, 71-73
Hotchner, A. E., 48-56, 167
"how" trap
  conventional "how" business
    views, 194-199
  definition of, 10-12
  escaping
    Fosbury Flop example, 12
    Home Depot case study, 8-10
    "how" versus "what," 199-201
    redundant ZIP Code data
      purchase example, 19-20
    Toshiba laptop repair time
      example, 21
    value of rethinking, 13-18
Hullabaloo, 159
Hyatt Hotels & Resorts, 165

I

Identify-and-Manage-Key-
  Suppliers "what" (Newman's
  Own), 54
Identify-Charity-Recipient "what"
  (Newman's Own), 55
identifying "whats"
  Alcoa case study, 41-48
  Newman's Own case
    study, 48-56
  questions to ask, 56-60

information technology (IT), 6
ING DIRECT, 118-132
  acquisition of NetBank
    assets, 130
  Create-New-Product/Service
    "what," 127
  Deliver-Product/Service
    "what," 123
  Fulfill-Demand "what," 125
  Generate-Demand "what," 122
  Manage-Capital-Assets
    "what," 125
  Manage-Human-Resources
    "what," 124
  Manage-Information-
    Technology-Services
    "what," 124
  Manage-Transaction "what," 123
  mission statement, 129
  Mortgage-Lending "whats," 126
  Plan-and-Manage-the-Business
    "what," 124
  Process-Mortgage-Application
    "what," 127
  Sell-Product/Service "what," 129
  success and accomplishments,
    131-132
  Validate-Available-Funds
    "what," 128
  Withdraw-Funds "what," 128
ING Groep, 130. See also ING
  DIRECT
InnoCentive, 188
Innovate-Product "what" (Procter
  & Gamble), 186
Install-Toilet "what" (Eclipse

Aviation Corporation), 140
insurance quotes, creating, 195-199
  heat map, 204-205
Intrade, 110-114
IT (information technology), 6

J-K

Jarvis, Jeff, 80
JetBlue, 99-105
Jordan, Michael, 62-63
judging performance. *See*
  performance, evaluating

Kindle, 184-185
Kuhlmann, Arkadi, 119-131. *See also*
  ING DIRECT

L

Lafley, A. G., 186-192. *See also* P & G
  (Procter & Gamble)
laws. *See* compliance
Leonard, Stew, 52
Letterman, David, 102
Level 1 maps, 206-210
Level 2 maps, 210-212
Linden Lab, 183
Lin Yutang, 109
Lowe's, 9

M

MacAskill, Chris, 179
Manage-Brand "what" (Target), 65
Manage-Capital-Assets "what"
  (ING DIRECT), 125
Manage-Communications
  (JetBlue), 104-105

Manage-Finances "what" (Dell), 80
Manage-Human-Resources "what"
    Burgerville case study, 67
    ING DIRECT case study, 124
Manage-Information-Technology-
    Services "what" (ING
    DIRECT), 124
Manage-Partner-Relationships
    "what"
    Cranium case study, 165
    P & G (Procter & Gamble)
        case study, 188-189
Manage-Supplier "what"
    (Burgerville), 68
Manage-Supply-Chain "what"
    (Target), 64-66
Manage-Talent "whats" (Procter &
    Gamble), 191
Manage-Transaction "what" (ING
    DIRECT), 123
Mankiw, N. Gregory, 110
Mann, Al, 141
Manufacture-Product "what"
    Boeing case study, 93-99
    Chrysler case study, 92
    connectedness, 88
    Dell case study, 80
    Eclipse Aviation Corporation
        case study, 138-139, 142-144
    Hon Hai Precision Industry case
        study, 72
    Newman's Own case study, 53
maps
    heat maps
        example, 204-205
        reading, 201-205

Level 1 maps, 206-210
Level 2 maps, 210-212
traditional workflow process
    maps, 194-199
Mark, Barry, 180
Markezich, Ron, 2-6
maturity, 203
McDonald's, 47-48
Mears, Tom, 70
measuring performance.
    See performance
Mees, Charles, 100
Merck & Company, 82-87
MFDs (multifunction displays), 145
Mizrahi, Isaac, 64
Moorad, Jeffrey, 65
Mortgage-Lending "whats" (ING
    DIRECT), 126
MTurk (Amazon Mechanical
    Turk), 182-183
multifunction displays (MFD), 145

N

Nardelli, Robert L., 8-10
NBA (National Basketball
    Association), 62
Neeleman, David, 102
NetBank, 130
Newman, Paul, 48-56, 167
Newmans.com, 53
Newman's Own, 48-56
Newman's Own Foundation, 55
Nike, 174
NineSigma, 188
Nordstrom, 58-59

O

O'Keefe, Georgia, 61
O'Neill, Paul, 41-48, 57
Oprah show, 164
O'Reilly Media, 184
O'Reilly, Tim, 184
Osama bin Laden, 110

P

Palmer, Arnold, 169
Paratek Pharmaceuticals, 85
parent/child relationships, 210
Pay-Employees "what," 88-89
Pell, Barney, 179
Perdew, Joe, 65
performance, evaluating, 202
    Burgerville case study, 66-71
    Hon Hai Precision Industry case
        study, 71-73
    Michael Jordan example, 62-63
    questions to ask, 73-75
    Target case study, 64-66
Perkins, Donald S., 46
P & G (Procter & Gamble), 186-192
    Create-New-Product "what," 187
    Evaluate-Innovation "what," 189
    Innovate-Product "what," 186
    Manage-Partners-Relationships
        "what," 188-189
    Manage-Talent "whats," 191
    Research-and-Develop-Product
        "whats," 187-188
    Research-Market-Trends
        "what"," 190-191
Pieper, Roel, 148
Plan-and-Manage-the-Business
    "what" (ING DIRECT), 124

Pogo Jet, 149
Powerset, 179
predictability
    Boeing case study, 93-99
    Chrysler case study, 92
    evaluating, 203
    JetBlue case study, 99-105
    limiting risk/maximizing
        benefit, 105-107
Prepare-Product "what" (Domino's
    Pizza), 59
Prepare-Quote "what," 204-205
*The Principles of Scientific
    Management* (Taylor), 31
processes as units of analysis, 33-34
process maps, 194-199
Process-Mortgage-Application
    "what" (ING DIRECT), 127
Process-Returned-Merchandise
    "what" (Nordstrom), 58
Procter & Gamble. *See* P & G
Propstra, George, 68, 70
Pruzan, Allen, 158

R

Raburn, Vern, 134-149. *See also*
    Eclipse Aviation Corporation
reading heat maps, 201-205
Recruit-New-Talent "what"
    Burgerville case study, 67
    Cranium case study, 165-166
reengineering, 34
regulations, compliance with. *See*
    compliance
Research-and-Develop-Product
    "whats" (Procter & Gamble),
    187-188

Research-Market-Trends "what" (Procter & Gamble), 190-191

Resolve Customer-Questions/ Problems "what"
   Alcoa case study, 57
   Dell case study, 79-82

Rip, Peter, 183

Roberts, Julia, 164

Rogue Creamery, 68

Rubin, Michael, 129

S

S3 (Simple Storage Service), 179

SaaS (software-as-a-service), 36

safety, Alcoa, 41-47

Sakkab, Nabil Y., 187, 190, 192

Sarbanes-Oxley Act of 2002, 112

Schedule-Flight-Crew "what" (JetBlue), 104

Schedule-Flight "what" (JetBlue), 103

Schultz, Howard, 163

Second Life, 183

Select-Charity "what" (Newman's Own), 55

Sell-Books "what" (Amazon.com), 173-174

Sell-Game "what" (Cranium), 164

Sell-Product "what"
   ING DIRECT case study, 129
   Newman's Own case study, 53

service-oriented architecture (SOA), 4, 36

787 Dreamliner (Boeing), 93-99

Shakespeare, William, 170

Simple Storage Service (S3), 179

Smith, Adam, 28-30

SmugMug Inc., 179

Snavely, Heather, 166

SOA (service-oriented architecture), 4, 36

software-as-a-service (SaaS), 36

Software Plus Services (S+S), 5, 87

Source-Raw-Materials "what" (Burgerville), 67

SOX (Sarbanes-Oxley Act of 2002), 112

Starbucks, 163

Stevens, Dennis, 5

Stewart, Martha, 52

Stiebrs Farms, 68

Stifel, Nicolaus & Company, 185

sustainability projects, Burgerville case study, 66-71

T

Tait, Richard, 150, 152-167. *See also* Cranium

Target, 64-66

Target Commercial Interiors (TCI), 64-66

tasks as unit of analysis, 28-30

Taylor, Frederick Winslow, 31

TBR (Technology Business Research), 80

TCI (Target Commercial Interiors), 64-66

Technology Entrepreneurs Network, 189

Test-Prototype "what" (Cranium), 156

Tillamook Creamery Association, 66

Toray Industries, 94

Toshiba, 21

TQM (total quality management)
    programs, 28
Train-New-Pilot "what" (Eclipse
    Aviation Corporation), 146
transparency, Eclipse Aviation
    Corporation, 147-149
Treebeard Books, 181
Trendsetter Award (Foodservice
    Consultants Society
    International), 70

U

units of analysis
    departments, 32-33
    processes, 33-34
    tasks, 28-30
    "whats," 34-38
    workers, 31
Unlawful Internet Gambling
    Enforcement Act, 111

V

Validate-Available-Funds "what"
    (ING DIRECT), 128
value
    definition of, 40
    evaluating, 202
Verify-Product-Quality "what"
    (Newman's Own), 54-55
Vioxx, 84
VLJ (Very Light Jet), 134
Vought Aircraft, 99

W

The Wealth of Nations (Smith), 28
Web 2.0, 4
"whats" (business capabilities). *See
    also specific "whats" (for example,
    Apply-Safety-Clothing "what")*
    Amazon.com case study, 169-186
        Amazon Web Services, 178-183
        Develop-Software "what,"
            177-178
        Distribute-Products "what,"
            176-177
        Fulfill-Orders "what," 173
        Kindle, 184-185
        Sell-Books "what," 173-174
    business value
        definition of, 40
        evaluating, 202
    compared to "how," 199-201
    compliance
        *analyzing legal status of
            "whats," 115-116*
        case study: Intrade, 110-114
        evaluating, 203
        *importance and impact on
            business, 112-114*
        *matching laws and "whats,"
            114-115*
    connectedness
        Dell case study, 78-82
        evaluating, 202
        *importance and impact of
            connections, 88-90*
        *Merck & Company case study,
            82-87*

Cranium case study, 152-167
  Analyze-Gamer-Interaction
    "what," 156
  Analyze-Gamer-Reaction
    "what," 156, 161
  Create-New-Game "what,"
    154-160
  Create-Prototype "what," 156
  Distribute-Game "what," 164
  Distribute-Product "what," 162
  Generate-Demand "what,"
    163-165
  Manage-Partner-Relationships
    "what," 165
  Recruit-New-Talent "what,"
    165-166
  Sell-Game "what," 164
  success and accomplishments,
    167-168
  Test-Prototype "what," 156
Eclipse Aviation Corporation
  case study, 134-149
  Assemble-Fire-Extinguisher
    "what," 146
  Assemble-Instrument-Panel
    "what," 145
  Connect-Skin-to-Skeleton
    "what," 143, 145
  Create-New-Product
    "what," 144
  Fabricate-Tail-Assembly
    "what," 142
  Install-Toilet "what," 140
  Manufacture-Product "what,"
    138-139, 142-144
  success and accomplishments,
    149-150

  Train-New-Pilot "what," 146
  transparency, 147-149
heat maps
  example, 204-205
  reading, 201-205
identifying
  Alcoa example, 41-48
  Newman's Own
    example, 48-56
  questions to ask, 56-60
ING DIRECT case study,
  118-132
  acquisition of NetBank
    assets, 130
  Create-New-Product/Service
    "what," 127
  Deliver-Product/Service
    "what," 123
  Fulfill-Demand "what," 125
  Generate-Demand "what," 122
  Manage-Capital-Assets
    "what," 125
  Manage-Human-Resources
    "what," 124
  Manage-Information-
    Technology-Services
    "what," 124
  Manage-Transaction
    "what," 123
  mission statement, 129
  Mortgage-Lending
    "whats," 126
  Plan-and-Manage-the-
    Business "what," 124
  Process-Mortgage-Application
    "what," 127

Sell-Product/Service
  "what," 129
success and accomplishments,
  131-132
Validate-Available-Funds
  "what," 128
Withdraw-Funds "what," 128
Level 1 maps, 206-210
Level 2 maps, 210-212
maturity, 203
overview, 2-5
parent/child relationships, 210
performance, evaluating, 202
  Burgerville case study, 66-71
  Hon Hai Precision Industry
    case study, 71-73
  Michael Jordan example, 62-63
  questions to ask, 73-75
  Target case study, 64-66
P & G (Procter & Gamble)
  case study, 186-192
  Create-New-Product
    "what," 187
  Evaluate-Innovation
    "what," 189
  Innovate-Product "what," 186
  Manage-Partners-
    Relationships "what," 188-189
  Manage-Talent "whats," 191
  Research-and-Develop-
    Product "whats," 187-188
  Research-Market-Trends
    "what", 190-191

predictability
  Boeing case study, 93-99
  Chrysler case study, 92
  evaluating, 203
  JetBlue case study, 99-105
  limiting risk/maximizing
    benefit, 105-107
  as units of analysis, 34-38
Withdraw-Funds "what" (ING
  DIRECT), 128
workers as unit of analyis, 31
workflow process maps, 194-199
WTO (World Trade
  Organization), 113

Y-Z

YourEncore network, 189

ZIP code case study, 19-20
Zocor, 82, 84
Zooreka, 165

FINANCIAL TIMES

In an increasingly competitive world, it is quality
of thinking that gives an edge—an idea that opens new
doors, a technique that solves a problem, or an insight
that simply helps make sense of it all.

We work with leading authors in the various arenas
of business and finance to bring cutting-edge thinking
and best-learning practices to a global market.

It is our goal to create world-class print publications
and electronic products that give readers
knowledge and understanding that can then be
applied, whether studying or at work.

To find out more about our business
products, you can visit us at www.ftpress.com.